Educating against drug abuse

Educating against
drug abuse

Unesco

Published in 1987 by the United Nations Educational,
Scientific and Cultural Organization
7 place de Fontenoy, 75700 Paris
Typeset by Unesco
Printed by Presses Universitaires de France, Vendôme

ISBN 92-3-102479-5
French version: 92-3-202479-9
Spanish version: 92-3-302479-2

Printed in France

Preface

Problems related to the use of legal and illegal drugs are gradually affecting children, young people and adults in both developing and industrialized countries: they constitue a threat to the health of the population and can damage the economic, even political, stability of nations. Many of the organizations within the United Nations system[1] have been mobilized to tackle this danger, working particularly on the repression of illicit trafficking, crop substitution and the reduction of demand.

With respect to Unesco, it has prepared an education and communication programme for the prevention of drug abuse. Its action concerning legal and illegal drug use related problems started in 1971 after adoption of Resolution 1,202 by the sixteenth session of the General Conference of Unesco requesting the Director-General 'to develop . . . a programme of study and action, at both national and international levels . . . aimed at promoting the contribution of social-science research, education and the media of mass communication to the solution of the problems of drug abuse'.

An initial publication, entrusted to Dr Helen Nowlis (United States of America) covered the subject as a whole in a methodical and dispassionate way, and identified the role of education in prevention. This study, entitled *Drugs Demystified*,[2] has been published in ten languages with several reprints. On the basis of the guidelines which it contains, a number of educators

enthusiastically undertook to incorporate the concept of prevention into their teaching activities. Many of those responsible for education, teaching and groups of young people and adults, however, wished to have some practical examples and information on experiments tried out in various countries, in short, to benefit from a training in prevention.

In an attempt to meet the requirements of educators, Unesco has compiled this new publication which contains most of the knowledge gained by the Organization in this area, together with examples of activities carried out by various countries, illustrating what it has helped to achieve. *Educating against Drug Abuse* is thus situated within the general context of prevention, and also tackles the delicate issue of evaluating preventive action.

Unesco entrusted production of this book to Dr Pierre Angel (France), psychiatrist at the Centre Médical Marmottan in Paris and Professor at the University of Paris VII, who is the author of Chapters 1 and 4, and to Nicole Friderich (Switzerland), from 1972 to 1983 responsible for Unesco's education programme concerning drug-use related problems, who is author of Chapter 2. Chapter 3 was provided by Etienne Brunswic, acting director of the Division of Educational Sciences, Contents and Methods of Education at Unesco.

Nicole Friderich also examined the ample documentation available in the Secretariat in order to provide a selection of examples. These had necessarily to be limited, which implied making some difficult choices.

This book is addressed to those responsible for education, particularly to the specialists in programmes involving the various disciplines concerned with preventive action, as well as all those who undertake preventive action against the abuse of legal or illegal drugs at the level of an administrative district, a teaching institution, an association, or even a class or group of young people or adults.

It was produced with the assistance of the United Nations Fund for Drug Abuse Control (UNFDAC), in accordance with a resolution of the twenty-third session of the General Conference of Unesco and is intended as a contribution to the International Conference on Drug Abuse and Illicit Trafficking, organized by the United Nations in Vienna in June 1987.

Unesco would like to thank all those who kindly gave permission for the inclusion of their texts, slightly altered or in resumé, in annex to this book.

The authors are responsible for the choice and the presentation of the facts contained in this book and for the opinions expressed therein, which are not necessarily those of Unesco and do not commit the Organization.

NOTES

1. United Nations Division of Narcotic Drugs (UNDN)
   United Nations Fund for Drug Abuse Control (UNFDAC)
   International Narcotics Control Board (INCB)
   World Health Organization (WHO)
   International Labour Office
   Food and Agricultural Organization of the United Nations (FAO)
   United Nations Industrial Development Organization (UNIDO)
2. Helen Nowlis, *Drugs Demystified: Drug Education,* 3rd ed., Paris, Unesco, 1982, 108 pp.

Contents

IV. *Three experiments evaluated*

1. Prevention of drug dependence: a Utopian dream?

The reports on drug abuse regularly drawn up for the international community are alarming: most of the indicators are on Red Alert. Consumption of psychotropic substances, that is, substances that alter the psyche, is rising constantly. Media campaigns are aimed chiefly at illicit drugs: the opiates, and in particular heroin, cannabis and cocaine.

Over the past twenty years addiction to both legal and illegal drugs has spread enormously, and now represents a serious public health problem. Drug use is no longer restricted to small minority and fringe groups; it is becoming commonplace. Many theories have been put forward to explain this phenomenon in society. One explanation lays emphasis on the social crisis factor, the calling into question of traditional values and the extent of socio-economic inequality. The violent upheavals (wars or economic disasters) that have shaken most countries of the world over the past twenty-five years seem in many cases to have damaged the control mechanisms that all societies possess to regulate their members' behaviour. In the industrialized countries, for example, hallucinogenic drugs are no longer regarded as one means of access to the supernatural, which the human soul can also reach, according to many different societies' interpretations, through the dream state. The psychadelic trip no longer takes place within a clearly structured social setting.

While the recent spread of drug dependence has been going on, psycho-pharmacologists (research scientists specializing in medicines for the treatment of mental states) have discovered powerful psychotropic substances which have revolutionized the treatment of mental illness. Drugs to treat anxiety, depression, delirium and hallucinations have been developed and prescribed for ever growing numbers of patients.

Tranquillizer consumption is extensive at the present time. Self-medication, too, is widespread. Some ill-informed parents of children who are boisterous or sleep badly give them tranquillizers or a sedative linctus without prescription.

Several surveys conducted in Western countries have shown that subjects who later become addicted to drugs frequently come from families in which the use of psychotropic drugs, with or without a doctor's prescription, is far more frequent than in the ordinary population.[1]

Canadian sociologists have even shown that the type of drugs used by the father or mother is often the same as that to which the son or daughter becomes addicted.[2]

The consumption of psychotropic drugs for non-medical purposes is reaching worrying proportions. Several different families of drugs are used. Barbiturates, which produce a state of intoxication and sometimes result in coma; amphetamines, which can lead to severe psychiatric problems; and tranquillizers in massive doses, which leave the subject morosely passive.

Pharmacologists are constantly developing molecules that can be diverted from their normal purposes by drug abusers seeking new sensations. Examples are the synthetic heroins, chemical hallucinogens, cocaine-based compounds, etc.

There is no limit to the curiosity of some adolescents in their quest for new drugs. This can be seen in the abuse of volatile solvents: young people inhale a wide range of substances from glues and petrol to varnishes and lacquers.

Nor must the role of alcohol be underestimated in this brief rundown of drugs. Production and consumption of alcoholic beverages are on the increase, not only in most industrialized countries but also in many Third World countries where social taboos are losing their force.

As to tobacco, its use is spreading internationally and few regions of the world have escaped this spread. It is clear that tobacco breeds dependence, that it can cause severe physical damage to smokers and that its use is sufficiently widespread to constitute a real public health problem. However, it differs from the major drugs in that it produces only a relatively slight stimulation or depression of the central nervous system and only quite slight changes in perception, mood, thinking, behaviour and motor function. Even at high doses, its psychotoxic effects are slight compared with those of the major drugs. Nonetheless, tobacco consumption is such that the World Health Organization (WHO) has adopted a resolute attitude: 'The cigarette is an instrument of death, with respect to which neutrality is no longer possible.'

All these drugs can lead to dependence, that is, to a psychic and physical state resulting from the interaction between a living organism and a substance. The characteristics of dependence are behavioural changes and other reactions which always include an impulse to continue taking the drug, either continually or periodically, in order to repeat its psychic effect and sometimes to avoid the unpleasant effects of withdrawal. A single individual may be dependent on one or several substances.

Fortunately, many subjects' encounters with drugs are brief and without consequence;

they take them out of curiosity, a taste for risk-taking or pressure from a peer group. For others, drug use is an occasional affair; this type of drug use is referred to as recreational: the consumer, adolescent or adult, normally uses the substance to procure immediate pleasure, to reduce the pain of anxiety and nervous tension or of a depressive life-experience, or to make it easier to integrate into a social group. Cannabis derivatives and alcohol in particular are often used in this way, only certain more vulnerable subjects going on through the stages that lead to dependence.

A great many different factors explaining the passage from occasional or recreational use to dependence have been brought to light.

A given individual's dependence on a given substance occurs as the combined result of three sets of factors.

First is the subject's personal characteristics and antecedents. Drug addicts are generally vulnerable adolescents who as children have presented numerous behavioral or personality disorders. Their life histories are marked almost inevitably by desertion, broken relationships or excessive emotional attachments. There are few who have not experienced failure at school or in their careers.

Second is the nature of the drug user's socio-cultural environment in general and of his or her family background in particular. Certain types of drug dependence are more widespread in certain easily identified more or less marginal social groups, whether economically privileged or underprivileged. Solvents, for example, are generally sniffed by young people in precarious financial situations, while cocaine has been used for many years by celebrities in the business world, show business and the arts. Social background has a profound influence on the drug addict's development as does family background, which often shows the same features: frequent personality disorders in the parents, excessive use of alcohol or psychotropic medicinal drugs coupled with acute problems inherent in the parent-child relationship.

The third factor is the pharmacodynamic properties of the substance in question, taking into account the quantity taken, frequency of use and whether taken orally, inhaled or injected.

In the face of the scale of drug abuse as a social phenomenon, the international community has moved into action. As N. Friderich shows, several international agencies are conducting action programmes against drug dependence. These institutions are trying to promote the gathering of reliable information on the extent and nature of the use of psychotropic drugs.

Most of the surveys undertaken are attempts to assess the consumption of psychotropics using large population samples. Most of the data come from studies carried out within the industrialized countries, but some developing countries are also beginning to undertake systematic studies of the question.

Several methods are used to supply quantitative and qualitative data on drug abuse.

The supply side of legal psychotropic drugs is assessed from figures supplied by the international control agencies, the pharmaceutical laboratories and health ministries; the supply side of illegal drugs is assessed through the quantities seized by police and customs and through surveys among the population at large.

The distribution of psychotropic drugs is assessed using doctors' prescription registers, surveys among dispensing chemists, studies of medicinal drug consumption in hospitals and clinics, etc.

Additional information comes from other sources: public health reports on diseases sometimes connected with drug addiction (for example, hepatitis and acquired immune deficiency syndrome - AIDS), statistics on overdose deaths and the annual reports of addiction treatment units and drug-education centres.

Much research has been done on the social problem connected with psychotropic drug use and abuse. Attempts are being made, for example, to evaluate the role of certain drugs, particularly alcohol, in road accidents. Surveys are being carried out on crime connected with the traffic in certain particularly costly drugs and others which modify behaviour and exacerbate the drug-taker's aggressive impulses.

Other studies have been devoted to the socio-economic cost of drug abuse: a fall in the user's productivity, treatment costs, funds taken up by policing, damage caused by acts of delinquency, etc.

The international agencies are increasingly encouraging data gathering on the consumption of psychotropic drugs. Standardized survey methods have been developed to facilitate country-to-country comparisons and provide a scientific basis for the action programmes to be undertaken.

In the face of a massive growth in drug use, defining and adopting a coherent policy covering all prevention, control and treatment activities are becoming increasingly necessary internationally. It is important, if short-term failure is to be avoided, to take account of the diversity of socio-cultural environments existing in each country and, indeed, in each region. It is the role of the international agencies to foster a pooling of knowledge and experience to avoid the duplication of errors already committed in some countries. It has, for example, proved largely unworkable to transpose the prevention techniques used in Western countries to Third World situations.

The budgets provided for prevention are very small compared to those provided every year for repression and the drive to reduce supply. The United Nations Fund for Drug Abuse Control (UNFDAC) figures for 1986 are as follows:

Budget approved:	21.4 million dollars

Percentage of funds per branch of activity	
Reduction of illegal supply	51
Control reinforcement	24
Reduction of illegal demand	13
Research	1
Other budget items	11

However, a number of studies suggest that the preventive approach should not be neglected in favor of repression or treatment. Repression, aimed at reducing supply by combating the production and sale of addictive drugs, runs up against numerous obstacles, political and socio-economic.

The therapeutic approach is a very delicate problem for a number of reasons.

Effective treatment requires the drug addict's active participation, whereas in fact he or she often shows a highly ambivalent attitude to the treatment programme. Because of the complexity of the problems posed by drug abuse, many treatment structures are needed, taking full account of the diversity of behaviour patterns found among drug addicts: detoxification units, post-cure centres, therapeutic communities, special dispensaries, employment rehabilitation workshops. The therapeutic programmes demand long, patient effort on the part of both the addict and those caring for him or her. Of course, the range of services offered and the type of intervention will vary from one country or region to another. Moreover, the therapeutic arsenal must adapt continually to a constantly changing situation: modification, for example, in the types of drugs being used (new drugs, or a fashion for this or that substance) or in the method of consumption (a shift from oral to intravenous administration).

Evaluations of treatment programmes for heroin addicts in particular are often disappointing: many addicts break off their treatment in mid-term or slip back shortly after the end of the cure. Only a minority (published figures are generally around the 30 per cent mark) break out of the drug's grip and succeed in completing their rehabilitation.

Given the limited efficacy of repressive and therapeutic measures alike, those with national responsibility in this field have adopted a wide variety of prevention policies. Here, it should be noted, a distinction is drawn between different levels of prevention:

Primary prevention, aimed at preventing the occurrence of a disorder, process or problem.

Secondary prevention, aimed at recognizing a disorder, process or problem and then suppressing it or modifying it in a positive way and as quickly as possible.

Tertiary prevention, aimed at delaying or preventing the further development of a disorder, process or problem and its after-effects even while the situation that gave rise to it is still present.

In fact, a prevention programme may have several effects: for example, effective tertiary prevention measures helping confirmed drug addicts to rehabilitate themselves will also have a primary prevention effect, since it will reduce proselytism and hence the spread of addiction. Rather than aiming at preventing or reducing the use of drugs as such, the overall end purpose of prevention must be to prevent the problems connected with the non-medical use of drugs or to reduce their incidence[3] and severity.

Epidemiological data[4] enable us to pinpoint those groups and individuals most at risk of drug dependence. This method of research provides information on the use of medicinal drugs, tobacco and alcohol, and on subjects' attitudes to illegal drugs. Epidemiological surveys bring out the characteristics of high-risk subjects and the interactions between different deviant behaviour patterns quite well.

The conclusions of most of these studies agree: confirmed drug addicts are for the most part individuals who have been rendered fragile by painful family events and a traumatic experience of human relationships.

Drug use can be increased by certain rapid changes in the nature of social constraints which result, for example, from migration or from socio-cultural change (uncontrolled urbanization).

It is understandable that, given the need to take into account the many different factors brought into play by drug-abuse behaviour, a very wide range of prevention strategies is called for. Among these, drug information and education campaigns hold pride of place.

One Unesco report clearly establishes the difference between the information and education approaches:

'*Drug information* is a form of communication which simply imparts factual knowledge or transmits cognitive learning. It is a fairly limited process in which the main elements are usually information concerning the drugs themselves and their [harmful] effects on people, along with instruction regarding specific drug-control legislation and other forms of social control. *Drug education*, on the other hand, is a broad range of concerted activities relating to teaching/learning situations and experience which attempts to maximize opportunities for the intellectual, emotional, psychological and physiological development of young people.'[5]

Information programmes were widely developed and used during the 1970s as it was thought that repeated warnings as to the harmful effects of drugs would make it possible to halt the spread of drug dependence. In fact it was soon noticed that information campaigns change the state of knowledge but do not change behaviour. It has been observed that sensationalism and the 'strategy of fear' make high-risk behaviour attractive to some young people and increases their experiments in drug-taking.

To attain its objectives, therefore, information must meet certain criteria. Only credible information, clear and properly adapted to its target audience, can have a favourable influence. The content of such education will differ, in particular as a function of its target: adolescents, their parents, health workers or various other professionally involved people. This is one of the reasons why many specialists are reticent towards any systematic use of the media to reach a very wide audience. Where this approach is used, they recommend a complementary programme to develop critical attitudes among young people towards certain negative influences in the media.

This example gives a good sense of the need to shift from information to education, that is, from the acquisition of knowledge to the learning of new patterns of behaviour.

We cannot here present an exhaustive list of the many prevention campaigns run over the past twenty years, but we shall stress a few general principles underlying many of these programmes. Prevention concerns all members of a society: not be a monopoly of certain specialists (general practitioners, psychiatrists, teachers or therapists), it must involve the whole community.

Drug abuse is one way, in which the malaise of a confused and disordered society is expressed. This type of deviant behaviour is in fact very often intricately interlinked with various other manifestations of suffering or failure to adapt: suicide, delinquency, violence and rejection of all integration into school or working life.

Prevention must thus be all-embracing. It must be aimed at improving the well-being of all the members of a given community. Prevention campaigns must not only reach the most vulnerable, but all those who are a part of their emotional and social surroundings: parents, teachers of all kinds. Educational programmes aimed at the young and those aimed at the surrounding community must be closely co-ordinated. It is at the local level that concerted action by all those involved proves to be most effective.

Lastly, the ethical concerns of those taking part in a prevention campaign must be regarded as being of prime importance. In particular, vigilance is needed to avoid the negative effects of certain interventions that may run counter to the defined objectives.

Preventive education must in no event bring social control to the forefront by accentuating the stigmatization of drug users; this will only push them irreversibly beyond the fringe.

It is by keeping to these basic principles that drug education will be able to play its rightful part in the fight against drug abuse.

NOTES

1. F. Davidson and M. Choquet, *Les lycéens et les drogues licites et illicites*, Paris, Institut National de la Santé et de la Recherche Médicale (INSERM), 1980, 90 pp.
2. R.G. Smart, D. Fejer and D. White, *Drug Use Trends among Metropolitan Toronto Students: Study of Changes from 1968 to 1972*, Toronto, Addiction Research Foundation, 1972 (unpublished MS.); R.G. Smart and D. Fejer, Drug Users and their Parents: Closing the Generation Gap in Mood Modification, *Journal of Abnormal Psychology*, No. 79, 1972, pp. 153-60.
3. Incidence rate: the rate of appearance of a disease or other condition over a given period in a population exposed to risk.
4. Epidemiology: the study of distribution of a disease or morbid state in a population and the factors which influence such distribution.
5. Meeting on Education and the Prevention of Drug Abuse, Particularly in the Developed Countries, Paris, 1972, *Report*, p. 8, Paris, Unesco, 1973 (Document ED/MD/26).

2. A new programme at Unesco

In an international organization whose field of action, though broad, is clearly defined, education, science, culture and communication, it is unusual for a new programme to appear, apparently unrelated with its traditional concerns. This, however, is what happened in November 1970 when Unesco was entrusted with the task of addressing the drug-related problems.[1]

What had happened? Between 1960 and 1970, the major industrialized countries had become aware, with astonishment and growing concern, of the increase in the consumption of drugs considered illegal. The use of cannabis spread, as did that of drugs which had hitherto only been used to a limited extent; for example, heroin, amphetamines or LSD, became increasingly popular.

Worse still, users were not confined to fringe groups identified with reprehensible behaviour; they came from all levels of society, and were very often young people. The media's interest in the phenomenon soon had the undesirable result of promoting it. Virtually total ignorance about the evolution of the problem helped the drug 'myth' to appear and take root among the general public. It was at this time that certain governments announced that 'drugs' had become the number one problem in their countries.

International bodies had long been dealing with the drug problem: this was the case of the Division of Narcotic Drugs of the United Nations, for illegal drugs, or the WHO, for both illegal and legal drugs (alcohol, tobacco, medicines). But in order to tackle this growing danger, the United Nations[2] decided to appeal to the institutions within the United Nations family such as the Food and Agriculture Organization of the United Nations (FAO), the International Labour Office (work and vocational training) and Unesco whose mandates had not previously led them to deal directly with this problem, and a special fund, UNFDAC, was established.

On the basis of Resolution 2303 of the United Nations General Assembly, the United States delegation to the Sixteenth Session of the General Conference of Unesco, together with representatives of twenty Member States, proposed the immediate introduction in the 1971/72 Programme of ways in which the Organization could contribute to solving the problems of drug use, and their subsequent implementation (Resolution 1202).

Fifteen years later, though it still seems unusual to have this programme in Unesco, it is firmly established in the Organization's activities; today it is representatives of numerous African and Latin American countries who request its strengthening.[3]

At the end of the 1970s, however, although governments felt that Unesco should 'act', the shape this action should take remained undefined. Bearing in mind the Organization's traditional vocation, it was decided that this action could most usefully be carried out within the fields of education, the social siences and communication.

With respect to financing, this was assured in the first stage through contributions from UNFDAC. Although most of their funding was used for law enforcement and the control of illegal drug production, funds were also available for preventive work, relying on educational programmes, sociological research and the media.

TAKING STOCK

A major survey was undertaken in the countries which had proposed this 'drug programme' to Unesco. It was really essential to obtain information on the policies followed in this field, current legislation, educational programmes, social science research, press campaigns, publications, etc.

PRINCIPLES OF ACTION

As it had been decided to concentrate initial efforts on industrialized countries, a meeting was held in December 1972 to determine a plan of action.

A survey had shown that, on the one hand, little attention had been paid to preventive education in these countries and, on the other, and this was more serious, that certain kinds of warnings did not change behaviour and could prove counter-productive. In particular, the confusion sometimes made between different types of drugs, all shown in an equally fearful light, caused arguments to lose credibility, while details of the dangers involved could, paradoxically, attract certain individuals.

In December 1972, a number of very important principles for preventive education were agreed upon: first, the term 'drugs' would cover both socially accepted or even promoted drugs such as alcohol (in many countries), tobacco and common remedies, and illegal drugs prohibited by law, because 'societies and nations around the world have defined the use of certain substances by certain people for certain reasons as a problem.'[4]

A second principle stemmed from the first: that of never identifying drug problems as young people's problems. There are two reasons for this. First, drug users are young adults (18-29 years old) rather than adolescents. Second, legal drugs are widely used by adults, be it alcohol, tobacco, tranquillizers, stimulants or sleeping pills. Finally, producers of drugs, whether legal or illegal, are always adults. It was important moreover to clearly distinguish between information as such, whose effectiveness seemed limited, and education defined as 'a broad range of concerted activities relating to the teaching/learning situation and experience which attempts to maximize opportunities for the intellectual, emotional, psychological and physiological development of young people'.[5] The pressing need to clarify ideas and theories concerning drugs led to the publication by Unesco of the booklet *Drugs Demystified*, by Dr Helen Nowlis,[6] who, with Dr Claude Olievenstein, had been one of the consultants at that first meeting. In addition, documents, studies, posters and films concerning drugs were being gathered, providing the basis of an international documentation collection at Unesco.

YOUNG PEOPLE'S OPINION

During the 1972 meeting, clearly fruitful in proposals, it had been requested that young people's representatives, who were often mentioned but seldom had the opportunity to give their views, should be invited to attend. Participants should fulfil two conditions: to have worked personally either on the prevention of drug-use related problems or in treatment or after-care centres and not to have attended as yet an international conference on this subject. Their countries of origin were necessarily limited to those which had undertaken work on drug education, prevention or information or which had established structures for assistance. These 'young people from industrialized countries', meeting at Sèvres (France) in 1973, showed a new way to prevention. They strongly opposed the tendency to consider drug use as an illness and users often as mentally sick (were they not very often received in psychiatric hospitals?) They also criticized the attitude of the media, in particular the press, and their contributions to the coining of the term 'drug scourge' which made the phenomenon appear as a punishment, incomprehensible and inevitable. Several of these young people, considering drug use no more than one of the indications of a deeper problem, well rendered by the title of a film produced by some of them for the meeting: *La drogue à sa place*[7] anticipated that if these problems were not remedied, they would gradually develop into increased violence.

The young people at the Sèvres meeting also requested that research be undertaken in various areas: (a) how the youth press talks about drugs (in four countries); (b) what happens to former drug users after treatment; (c) what is the community approach to these problems; and (d) how to assess preventive education.

SPECIFY AND CLARIFY

At the same time, Unesco provided help for studies and meetings, so as to deal more directly with the problems of prevention in countries using the same language and whose education system were often close: Nordic countries, German and French-speaking industrialized countries. Ideas became clearer; it was recognized that preventive education action involved various social sectors: teachers, parents, young peoples' associations, community institutions. An isolated effort on the part of one of these groups was likely to produce incomprehension and failure; team-work was therefore suggested in which parents would join certain teachers, school nurses, administrative personnel and students, on a voluntary basis in the school context. Even certain misunderstandings proved to be a valuable source of information concerning the path to follow: the title of a meeting concerning education on drug-related problems *for* parents and teachers turned into 'Education . . . *by* parents and teachers'.

Meanwhile, Unesco's action evolved and became more clearly defined in two aspects: understanding the problem and the geographical extension of the programmes.

In the first place, problems had to be clarified and explained simply and dispassionately, although they were very complex issues, often producing deep-seated reactions. The short book by Helen Nowlis, a psychologist and educator,[8] met this need so well that new editions and translations were constantly produced (there are currently versions in ten different languages[9]) and over a decade later it remains a basic book for teachers.

In it one finds a clearly defined chapter on 'Drugs and drug effects'[10] (and not a mere catalogue of drugs under one heading or another) in which it is stated that 'Each tends to attribute to the substance itself characteristics that more properly belong to the interaction among substance [drug], organism [user] and context [socio-cultural environment].'[11]

Covering the subject of 'Drug use and drug users'[12] Dr Nowlis dispels the notion of 'drug addicts', an undifferentiated group, on the one hand, and 'normal', or 'decent' people on the other; she distinguishes experimental use from casual or ocassional use, regular use and heavy or compulsive use.

While considering the various prevention strategies, the author asserts that 'Information alone indiscriminately given and passively received is of little value [as] Man has a habit of selectively attending to and believing only that which supports his current beliefs and justifies his current behaviour.'[13]

However good these strategies are, they are never universally valid or immutable, so it must be possible to adopt or even change them. 'People and institutions do not change easily. Ways of stating problems and ways of responding to them, tend, once accepted, to be pursued doggedly.'[14]

ACTION FOR THE THIRD WORLD

At another level, geographical in this case, Unesco was to extend its action to three regions which did not comprise any of the 'over-developed' countries. The latter were now in a position to continue their action on the basis of their own resources. Only one national project was to be undertaken, successfully, by Unesco, with the assistance of UNFDAC. This was in Portugal. It was not until 1980 that a new meeting of industrialized countries was held in Lisbon.

On the other hand, the attention of the United Nations was focused on several Asian countries. Among these, countries such as Thailand, Burma and Laos are producers of opium and its derivatives; others, like the Philippines or the territory of Hong Kong, are only users, but in a way which causes much concern.

Major programmes were launched to attempt to replace opium poppy cultivation by other agricultural activities (stock-breeding, coffee growing, production of essential oils, fruit, etc.) or handicrafts, in order to limit the production of illegal drugs at their origin. Naturally, the legal production of opium, restricted to certain countries, mainly India, continued under strict control, as a function of world demand for opium derivatives for medical purposes (morphine or codeine) which is transmitted yearly by governments to the United Nations International Narcotics Control Board.

These programmes for substituting agricultural production in fact required a community and rural development effort if they were to be adopted by the populations involved and if these were not to suffer from a loss of income.

While in Asia Unesco collaborated in activities aimed in particular at eliminating the supply of opium-derived drugs, in Latin America and Africa it launched activities attempting first to develop preventive education.

DRUGS IN LATIN AMERICA

Despite a certain number of common features, the countries of Latin America and the Caribbean form a far from homogeneous group.

National studies, undertaken with Unesco's assistance, highlighted the concern of certain governments but at the same time showed that most countries minimized the dangers of the situation.

There is nothing surprising about this reaction since the word 'drugs' usually causes unease, as if it were question of an illness, even a shameful illness. However, most of

the countries of the region were becoming aware of the harm caused by abuse of socially-accepted drugs, alcohol and tobacco in particular. In the Andes, the small red flag in an isolated dwelling indicating that alcoholic drinks were for sale was found far more often than the white flag which only indicated that food was served. Most of the Latin American countries and some Caribbean states therefore sent educators to a meeting organized by Unesco in Lima in January 1976. In order to improve the quality of the discussions, six had previously received travel fellowships enabling them to see what was already being done with respect to prevention in other countries in the continent, in North America and in Europe.

This process produced ideas rather than models. The discussions showed that many participants wished to see joint action undertaken by the countries of the region, although Caribbean educators clearly indicated that they wished their cultural differences to be respected. According to some participants, the traditional use in their countries of origin of certain plants from which are produced drugs proscribed by law and international agreements, such as coca or cannabis, had to be borne in mind. Peasants chew coca leaves as they would drink a coffee or take any other legal stimulant. The leaves produce the feeling of renewed energy and prevent hunger pangs. Tea is made from them to relieve altitude sickness, and this has always been the case. It is a very different application from that of taking cocaine as a drug. In some islands, cannabis is considered as a traditional cure for minor illnesses, a tonic when undertaking hard work and, in the religious context of one minority, as the 'weed of wisdom' whose carefully controlled use facilitates contact with the deity. This too is different from the addict's use of marijuana or hashish, the main products of cannabis whose trafficking and consumption are forbidden by law. All these are region-specific examples of the complexity of the problem.

In several countries, only a minority of children go to school, and most of those who do remain for a few years only. To reach the young people outside school and to be heard by those adults who cannot read, it was necessary to use out-of-school educational methods widely, together with much imagination.

Finally, the teachers who came to Lima called for practical measures and international assistance: if effective educational and preventive action was required, experiments had to be undertaken in the region to determine which methods gave the best results and which programmes, leaflets, posters or films best responded to the traditions and cultures of these countries. To launch this kind of undertaking, the assistance of Unesco and UNFDAC would clearly be necessary. Thus one year later, an experiment was started in Argentina, entitled DINEMS[15]/Unesco/FNUFUID[16], to run for five years. Two years later, two 'seminar-workshops' one in English, the other in Spanish, were organized for educators who undertook the study and production of 'educational material' in these two languages: teachers' manuals, model lessons, radio programmes, pamphlets, short video films, etc. Five of these countries then launched their own activities with the support of Unesco and UNFDAC.

THE ARGENTINE EXPERIMENT

A dual programme was undertaken in Argentina under the guidance of the Ministry of Education and with the enthusiastic prompting of a former Unesco fellow.

It consisted, on the one hand, of seeking volunteers from among secondary-school teachers to inform them and give them teaching guidelines. They were not specialists, but imaginative and inventive individuals motivated by the subject of prevention: teachers of history, geography, natural or social sciences, psychology or physical education. More *promotores de salud* (health promoters) than drug-abuse fighters, they were to work on developing positive attitudes towards a healthy life-style. The first team, trained in the capital, instructed in turn other teams in eighteen regions, with the help of teaching materials. This material concerned adolescents' psychology and the conditions under which an individual may be led to use either illegal or legal drugs; it also gave information about the drugs themselves and their effects.

On the other hand, two schools were chosen in 'high-risk' suburbs of the capital for a more intensive experiment which was to be closely followed, evaluated, and adapted according to results; in short, it would serve as a laboratory for trying out preventive education. In selected classes, certain teachers (*profesores consultores*) were responsible for the experiment and were to help their colleagues and students. Their task was to improve communication with the students, guide them, help them learn how to make decisions, particularly concerning drug use, and give them information whenever necessary. In a fairly short time, students themselves could be involved in preventive action (*pares consejeros*); they were chosen for their influence on their peers and their willingness to help them. Several information sessions were organized for them on the problems of adolescence, on ways to overcome certain difficulties and on drugs in current use. Here again, it was not drug-abuse fighters who were recruited, but young people anxious to help others to feel less alone and to overcome the difficulties they may be facing.

A series of teaching sheets were prepared entitled *El ABC de las drogas* to help teachers interested in drug problems; they could also be used by the students. Then a collection of teaching suggestions was published, entitled ¿*Qué hacer?* [What should be done?], followed by a collection of texts for young people and a compilation from experiments tried out in a large number of schools by the *promotores de salud*. This was packed with new ideas, from a 'project' concerning the household medicine cabinet (what it should and should not contain) to an anti-tobacco tune composed by the students, via the performance of short plays, a survey among the local population on cigarette smoking, etc. It was entitled ¿*Qué se esta haciendo?* [What is being done?]. The final brochure published was for parents: *Drogas en mi casa, jamás!* [Drugs at home, never!].

The intensive experiment was extended from the two pilot schools to twenty more schools, then to another fifty, and the results were made available to other Latin American and Caribbean countries during a new meeting held in 1982.

WHAT CAN BE DONE TO HELP CARIBBEAN EDUCATORS?

It was realized in Lima that the texts and audi-visual material available to those who wished to carry out preventive work was still limited and often inappropriate. It was usually imported from industrialized countries where living conditions were very different and was likely to produce negative reactions. In the two seminar workshops organized by Unesco in 1978, educators agreed on the goals they wished to achieve through preventive education and the type of 'educational materials' needed (written, visual, audiovisual); they immediately started to prepare some examples of what they wanted. Although time was insufficient to produce properly finished work during the workshop, the basic stimulus had been given and five countries later requested the assistance of Unesco and UNFDAC to continue the work started in their own way.

In Guyana, for instance, the National Commission for Unesco[17] undertook to supply guidelines on prevention to teachers, parents, educators and leaders of young people or adult groups. These guidelines consist of duplicated texts in a cardboard cover, simple, clear, rather short and centring on the situation in the country itself. They concern in particular the three main drugs used: alcohol, tobacco and cannabis, mention amphetamines and barbiturates (stimulants and depressants) and stress that medicines prescribed by doctors are useful drugs, provided that the user keeps to the prescription. The information brochure for educators specifies that its aims are to raise their awareness about drug-use related problems, to supply them with information and 'teaching aids' to train and guide their students, to show them how to introduce the subject into school programmes and to young people's groups, to guide them in their role of educators working on prevention and to suggest healthy and interesting activities they could organize for young people. The conclusion appeals to educators to put their

own houses in order: 'We all use drugs; let us learn to reduce our intake of medicines, alcohol and tobacco.' It also urges them to bear in mind the traditional use of certain substances in the country and its spread to new groups which no longer observe ancient precautions. A teacher's guide on drug use, to be used within the framework of health education programmes, is available for secondary-school teachers. Finally, a work unit establishes objectives for each term during the four years of secondary education (e.g. to examine the risks of self-medication, or to help students to acquire strength of character and decision-making skills) defines the teaching and learning content, and lists sources of information and materials available (written, audio-visual), as well as ways to evaluate the results of these efforts. Teachers are reminded that preventive education must be incorporated not only into health education, but also into history, geography, biology, science, physical education and domestic science.

A shorter version of the information brochure was prepared for parents and group leaders in the form of questions and answers (What is a drug? What is wrong with taking a drug if no one else is affected? What is the situation in Guyana?).

Finally, for both groups, and in order to raise the awareness of the general public, the National Commission of Guyana produced a video cassette of three one-act plays illustrating everyday situations, entitled *Drugs . . . Should I?* The text of these plays is also available, thus increasing the teaching value of the material.

CO-OPERATION WITHIN THE REGION

Experiences acquired in a given country can be very useful to its neighbours. Unesco has therefore often called on educators who have carried out interesting work, with or without its assistance, so that it can provide their collaboration to governments wishing to undertake a preventive programme with the support of the Organization.

In addition, Unesco has allocated fellowships to educators already working on preventive education 'projects' under its auspices to enable them to go and study the various methods used in other countries, their success and the difficulties encountered. Thus, a complete network of information and exchange is gradually developing.

DRUGS IN AFRICA?

An initial survey carried out in 1974 indicated that most African countries thought that drugs did not pose a serious problem to them, or even doubted the existence of a drug problem.

However, Sierra Leone requested preventive education action from Unesco. Kenya hosted several conferences on law enforcement or pharmacology. Cameroon organized seminars on alcoholism and related problems. Togo participated energetically in the work of the United Nations Commissionon Narcotic Drugs. Senegal already had a rather detailed legislation on the subject. Nigeria had published studies on drug use by secondary school students in Lagos. On Unesco's initiative, these six examined the state of preventive education in their countries, and met in Lomé (Togo) in September 1976.

As in Latin America, 1976 was to mark the beginning of specific action. What had the African educators meeting in Lomé found? The drug problem well and truly existed in Africa, or at least in certain countries. The consumption of alcohol, either locally produced or imported, continued to increase, with even more damaging effects on account of the climate. Tobacco, sometimes considered as the first luxury of Third World countries, was subject of a very important publicity and inducement campaign on the part of manufacturers: should not these populations, with as yet few smokers and generally none of the fears and prejudice *vis-à-vis* tobacco as in industrialized countries, be won over as quickly as possible to smoking? Cannabis, which grows particularly well in African climates and whose potency is appreciated by the connoisseur, was increasingly used by social or age groups (especially young people) very different from the dockers or labourers who traditionally used it. This situation was also far removed

from the controlled use of cannabis as a natural medicine. Other plants from the traditional pharmacopoeia, often powerful hallucinogens also used for the purpose of inititation, were no longer limited to these strictly controlled applications. They were taken without any precautions in the search for intoxication, for a trip. Finally, medicines posed a serious problem: owing to the inadequacy of the distribution network and control methods, they were sold in markets after being illegally imported or diverted from legal circulation.

On the other hand, some drugs which produced alarm in other places (such as morphine, heroin, cocaine or LSD) were virtually unknown, and it was preferable not to publicize them.

This was a situation well suited to preventive action, but it had to be done quickly. However, the educators who could be requested to help within and outside school were already overloaded; the incorporation of preventive education in their work had to be facilitated, the necessary texts and audiovisual materials made available to them and instruction given on its effective use. But these teaching aids did not exist in African countries, where the issue was being tackled for the first time. There was no question either of using material prepared for countries in other regions, with different traditions and cultures where other drugs were used. In Lomé it was argued that it was necessary to give due importance to the traditional African values and appeal to young people and adults to contribute to national development and that, furthermore, care should be taken to prevent through education the imitation of foreign fashions and patterns often related to the use of drugs.

Other African states started to be concerned about drugs. Twelve countries (six French-speaking and six English-speaking) formed working groups with the help of Unesco; some produced slides, others a teacher's guide, others an outline of a school programme, a film, etc. Two regional workshops, one in French and the other in English, worked on sample teaching material and produced model lessons and examples of role-playing and use of the press, posters, radio or slogans. With the help of Unesco and UNFDAC, six countries then undertook to develop and adapt what had been produced in the workshops and carried out experiments in preventive education.

Two methodology courses were organized, one in Gabon in 1981 and one in Kenya in 1983, to facilitate the field testing of these various teaching aids, thereby demonstrating the feasibility of a global approach for a given population through primary school, secondary school, out-of-school young people and adults. These courses were followed by educators from fifteen countries and three other countries were going to follow suit.

SCHOOL AND PREVENTION IN TOGO

Unfortunately, not all the projects undertaken in Africa can be described, but those carried out in Togo and Benin can be mentioned to illustrate two very different approaches.

In Togo, school education was chosen as the vehicle for prevention, due to the energetic prompting of a Minister of Education who, since 1976, had participated himself in the various meetings and African courses given by Unesco. An interdisciplinary commission studied the teaching programmes of the lower and upper secondary levels to see how knowledge (that is, information) and school activities producing a positive effect on the development of Togolese youth (training) could be incorporated into them. The most important element was the development of individuals able to look after themselves, to tackle their problems and to assume responsibility. It was a question of developing attitudes and behaviour not through inculcation but as a result of an effort of thought and analysis. Considerable information had to be given on the nature of drugs and problems related to their use to help students to form their own opinions on certain issues (health is a state of physical, mental and social well-being, the discriminating use of drugs and medicines can save lives, individuals should know how to take responsibility for their decisions) and to adopt positive and constructive attitudes.

Preference was given to active methods and these were used whenever possible, since behaviour cannot be shaped by words alone.

Preventive education, therefore, promoted in addition an opportunity for dialogue, discussion and individual or group activities, and contributed to updating teaching methods.

A two-week seminar was held for some twenty specialists to prepare the necessary teaching material. After revision, their work was published in two volumes for teachers (one for primary and lower secondary, the other for upper secondary) containing scientific and socio-psychological information, teaching suggestions and class material.

At the same time, a commission responsible for supervising the experiment produced material for evaluating, on the one hand, the teaching materials and methods suggested and, on the other, possible changes in attitudes and behaviour. Although the experiment was limited in the first stage to schools, a national seminar in Lomé offered teachers from all regions the opportunity to meet together with doctors, chemists and those responsible for the protection of young people, for juvenile courts, for national security and for the minors squad, to consider extending to the out-of-school environment and campaigns by the media.

Training the involved teachers was carried out through a series of seminars comprising three components: facts, studying available teaching material and programming classroom actions. Training included major activities, staggered throughout the year, which supplemented the lessons in the study programme as such (showing of the film *SOS Drogue*, poster competitions, surveys, the production of short plays, etc.) in order to avoid the prevention programme being forgotten during the school year.

A COMMUNITY APPROACH IN BENIN

In Benin, the preventive education programme was designed with the whole population as a target. This was possible on account of the administrative structures in neighbourhoods and villages. Each neighbourhood, commune or municipality has a communal revolutionary committee (CCR), a neighbourhood health complex (CSD) and a health committee (CS), and in each district or a village, there is a local revolutionary committe (CRL) and a health committee or a village health unit (CQS, UVS). These neighbourhood health committees were chosen to contribute to the prevention project. They were composed of two traditional healers, a teacher, an agricultural extension worker, a person responsible for social affairs (a member of the CRL), two CRL militants (prominent local figures), a health team and a person responsible for cultural affairs and literacy.

The out-of-school preventive education programme for adults and young people began with a very detailed study of the environment of the population selected for the first experimental stage, that of Cotonou (Cotonou VI), the economic capital of the country. A pre-tested and adapted questionnaire was given to a sample of 1,200 people by medical students. Analysis of the answers made it possible to specify objectives as a function of the situation and the needs of the targeted population. Educators/group leaders were trained in a series of seminars in which they were informed about the situation and problems in the various neighbourhoods (results of the survey), the various drugs used (mainly alcohol, tobacco, cannabis, certain local plants and some medicines) and the causes and effects of drug use from the psycho-sociological viewpoint.

Since activities foreseen included audio-visual methods in particular, a group of educators, using closed-circuit television, produced a number of short films showing certain problem situations highlighted by the survey; they provided a very stimulating basis for discussion during the meetings organized by the CQS in their neighbourhoods. The cultural officials and teachers foresaw theatrical activities illustrating significant situations, and groups of young people could think up activities in which they would be particularly involved, such as producing posters to be pasted up in the neighbourhood or undertaking cultural activities to replace evenings spent in the bar or on the beach, smoking and drinking.

At the same time, media campaigns to raise public awareness were envisaged for the population at large: regular television programmes for young people, production of shows and songs recorded on cassettes and disseminated during public gatherings,

organization of a poster competition offering prizes provided by local businesses, the dissemination of a small mimeographed newspaper in schools, clinics, etc.

WHAT OF THE ARAB STATES?

Are the Arab states concerned with the problems of drug use? Some consider that their legislation, together with the stipulations of Islam, that anything that causes intoxication in the broadest sense is forbidden to believers, is sufficient to ward off these problems. Others foresee educational measures. To help the latter to take stock of the situation, Unesco entrusted an Algerian sociologist and teacher with the task of collecting available information on the spot and producing a study.[18]

Travel grants enabled educators from the states so desiring to observe preventive methods in the education systems in other regions. Egypt obtained Unesco and UNFDAC assistance to undertake an in-depth survey in teaching institutions, to prepare a report for secondary-level educators and to organize an intensive seminar for some fifty teachers. Their conclusions, intended as a guide for fellow teachers, stress the essential role played by religious teaching, civic instruction and carefully-prepared information in prevention.

NEW PATHS IN ASIA

The work already being carried out through national programmes, in some Asian countries and the concerns of neighbouring countries induced Unesco to take the first step towards a field of action that it had not yet tackled, owing to lack of resources rather than failure to recognize its importance. It concerned the role that education could play in the social rehabilitation of those who had given up drug use and who, often viewed with disapproval, lacked the necessary training to get a job. Some had little or no schooling, and this was often one of the indirect reasons for their turning to drugs; others had dropped out of their studies because of problems stemming from drug use. Could completion of their education be an important contribution to their re-entry, and sometimes their first entry, into social life?

In 1977, Unesco made this question one of the two topics for consideration at a meeting of ten South-East Asian countries and, given the interest raised in those states which possessed treatment and disintoxication centres, Unesco held a meeting in 1980 in Hong Kong for educators from both industrialized countries (Australia and the United States) and Asian countries, from Pakistan to the Philippines, to study the role that education could and should play in social rehabilitation. It was agreed that education for the family and immediate circle of the former drug user was necessary, first, in order to ensure that he received the support he needed, and second, because it was considered that his 'social inadaptability' was caused not only by the harmful effects of drug intake but also by the disapproving attitude of society towards him on account of his drug use.

With Unesco and UNFDAC assistance, three countries undertook to test the conclusions reached in Hong Kong. In Thailand, for instance, a plan was drawn up to provide education and vocational training to people who had followed disintoxication treatment in a centre operating in the Buddhist monastery of Tam Kra Bok and to help them find a job so they could support themselves.

COLLABORATION BETWEEN INDUSTRIALIZED COUNTRIES

In the industrialized countries, preventive experiments evolved and exchanges increased towards the beginning of the 1980s, owing to Unesco's assistance. One method used in secondary schools in the Canton of Vaud, Switzerland, is based on the introduction of mediators, teachers who are given special training to meet the needs of students, teachers and parents with respect to drug-use problems, for three hours a week (when they were relieved of their usual work). The same method was launched in Portugal on the basis of advice from a Unesco consultant who went there on several occasions. This experiment

was carried out within the framework of the UNFDAC assistance project concerning legislation, preventive education and the treatment of drug users, and was even extended to prisons.

Portugal was also to host another meeting of industrialized countries which felt the need to take stock of the situation, eight years after the Paris meeting. Twenty-one of these countries had replied to a survey, which made it possible to outline the situation with respect to drug problems and prevention. In 1980, educators from twenty-two countries agreed on a certain number of basic principles to prevent or minimize all harmful use of drugs. Experience had shown that to concentrate efforts on urging people not to use drugs, and to hope that all drug use would be eliminated, was 'unrealistic, expecially in societies that accept virtually unrestricted consumption of alcohol and tobacco'. The educators proposed more modest but more realistic goals, both at individual and collective levels, and at the national policy level.

In order to establish global action, they urgently called for the co-ordination of school and out-of-school programmes, particularly through training experiences shared by those implementing these programmes. Owing to financing difficulties, evaluation became increasingly an essential element of these experiments.

One of the requests submitted at Lisbon was immediately accepted by Unesco. It concerned obtaining information from Member States on a maximum of six preventive education experiments effectively implemented in their countries, together with detailed documentation on the basic principles, objectives, approach, methods, material and evaluation of these programmes and an outline of the results achieved and the problems that had to be overcome. In 1981/82, some ten countries responded to the need for specific examples by sending detailed reports on the programmes actually implemented to Unesco which circulated and disseminated them.

This exchange enabled several countries to benefit from the experience of others, e.g. the Vaud Canton method by Portugal, and France in the shape of the *adultes-relais* system.

Development of operations in Africa

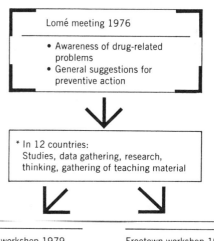

Lomé meeting 1976

- Awareness of drug-related problems
- General suggestions for preventive action

* In 12 countries:
Studies, data gathering, research, thinking, gathering of teaching material

Abidjan workshop 1979   Freetown workshop 1980
Côte d'Ivoire   6 countries   Sierra Leone   6 countries

- Definition of principles and objectives
- Review and description of teaching to be prepared
- Description of evaluation tools

- Implementation of workshop suggestions in various countries
- Preparation of teaching material
- Training of personnel
- Preparation of evaluation tools
- Testing

Methodology course 1981   Methodology course 1983
Libreville, Gabon   7 countries   Embu, Kenya   7 countries

- Field testing
- Whole population as target

* Project development
- National seminars for officials
- Revision of teaching material
- Preparation of longer term projects
- Incorporation of teaching programmes in teachers' colleges and institutions training social workers
- Improvement of evaluation tools

* Operations implemented at national level

ASSESSING PROGRESS

Since the need to evaluate projects under way was also felt in the Latin American and Caribbean countries, it was decided to take stock of the situation there too, and in July 1982, six years after the Lima meeting, the origin of their experiments, these countries sent educators to examine the most interesting programmes undertaken in the region, among which was that carried out in Argentina with Unesco and UNFDAC support. As agreement was quickly reached on the principles to be observed with respect to prevention, efforts concentrated on examining the difficulties faced by the pioneers who had undertaken preventive action and in finding ways to solve very specific problems such as financing pilot experiments, obtaining education officials' agreement to teachers' secondment, organization of educator-training courses and ways to exchange documentation.

WHAT NOW?

At present, preventive education efforts have increased despite the difficulties encountered. Many countries have requested Unesco's help for in-depth work, a slow, persevering task, and a true educational effort is being carried out. Paradoxically, it is sometimes the growing interest in drug-use related problems that represents a threat to this action.

Certain groups, media specialists, public figures or politicians, believing that they are acting appropriately and prompted by righteous indignation against trafficking and the profits made from illegal drugs, undertake campaigns which alarm the general public, demand repressive action and ignore the less-obtrusive action of educators or refuse to acknowledge its effectiveness. It is vital that Unesco pursue its action, with United Nations support, and that it continue to provide educators with specific ways to undertake effective prevention.

NOTES

1. Resolution 1202 which was adopted by the General Conference of Unesco at its

sixteenth session (Paris, 12 October to 14 November 1970).
'*Recognizes* that Unesco, as the educational agency of the United Nations System, has an important role to play in contributing to the solution of the problem of drug abuse . . . and
'*Urges* the Director-General, as funds become available, to develop . . . a programme of study and action, beginning in 1971 and extending over the 1971-76 period, aimed at promoting the contribution of social-science research, education and the media of mass communication to the solution of the problems of drug abuse.'

2. Resolution 2434 (twenty-third session, 24 September - 21 December 1968) of the United Nations General Assembly invited the United Nations specialized agencies to participate in the preparation of plans to help to solve drug-related problems.

3. Resolution 4.8 adopted by the General Conference of Unesco at its twenty-third session (Sofia, 8 October - 9 November 1985) on the initial proposal of fifteen African and four Latin American countries. '*Invites* the Director-General to undertake large-scale preventive action against the abuse of drugs and narcotics . . .' and '*Recommends* that this action should be pursued and developed and assigned greater priority and that Unesco's activities in the social sciences, communication and culture should contribute in substantial measure to programmes of action in this area.'

4. Helen Nowlis, *Drugs Demystified: Drug Education*, 3rd ed., p. 10, Paris, Unesco, 1982.

5. *Meeting on Education in More-Developed Countries to Prevent Drug Abuse, Paris, 1972. Report.* p. 11.

6. Nowlis, op. cit.

7. This film, *Delta Experience*, was produced by Unesco, with the aid of FNULA, in English, French and Spanish. It describes the drug problem among youth in Belgium and the methods used by the Delta Group.

8. Nowlis, op. cit.

9. English, French, Spanish, German, Arabic, Icelandic, Italian, Portuguese, Swedish and Thai.

10. Nowlis, op. cit., pp. 20-8.

11. Ibid., p. 20.

12. Ibid., pp. 30-7.

13. Ibid., pp. 40-4.

14. Ibid., p. 20.

15. National Office for Secondary and Higher Education

16. Spanish acronym for UNFDAC

17. A Commission exists in nearly all Unesco Member States, composed of national figures highly qualified in the areas of education, natural or social sciences, culture or communication, who are responsible for liaison with Unesco. Its Secretariat receives publications and correspondence from the Organization and collaborates in its activities.

18. C. Ougouag, *Study of Problems Relating to Drug use in the Arab Countries and the Role of Information and Education in Prevention*, Paris, Unesco, 1979 (EPDAR/1; ED/79/WS/1).

vive la santé !

je bois de l'eau, du lait, des jus de fruits.

COMITE NATIONAL DE DEFENSE CONTRE L'ALCOOLISME 20, RUE SAINT FIACRE 75002 PARIS

3. Developing a prevention strategy

Although educational activities play an important role in drug abuse prevention, they do not constitute a prevention strategy on their own.

Prevention of the abuse of legal or illegal drugs, whether alcohol, tobacco, solvents, psychotropic substances or narcotics, must be based on wide-ranging measures.

At the legislative level, international conventions and national laws are directed against the production, trading, distribution and consumption of illegal drugs.

As for the legal drugs, they, too, are subject to legislative, administrative or reglementary measures, such as rules on advertising, special conditions of sale (certain substances prohibited from sale to minors, restrictions on quantity and consumption prohibited or restricted in public places), special taxes on certain products, medical controls for specified activities such as sports events or certain professions (for example, pilots or taxi-drivers).

From a social point of view, the aim of prevention is to encourage associations of various kinds, in particular the efforts of voluntary bodies specializing in prevention work related to certain drugs (alcohol, psychotropic substances) and to open information guidance and counselling centres especially for 'high-risk' population groups.

Given that any programme of prevention also depends on a precise knowledge of the terrain, a thorough investigation into health and sociological and psychological situations and epidemiological studies are important to elicit factors capable of influencing consumption.

In the first place, preventive education must be integrated into an overall policy on drug abuse prevention, of which it is one component. The policies on prevention, however, vary from country to country and, within a particular country, profound differences often exist between the various subcultures and communities which call for different approaches to the problem. This rules out a universally acceptable model of prevention and makes any action that has proved effective in one context at one moment difficult to transplant. As Helen Nowlis[1] remarks, 'international discussions always produce confrontations in which the citizen from "x" says "that cannot possibly work in my country because this is how the schools (the family, the church, the government, the youth club, the youth themselves) understand and do things".'

In education, preventive action raises complex issues. First, as we have just seen, it forms one of a whole series of preventive measures affecting many different areas;[2] at the same time, it must adapt to the characteristics of the education system within which it is pursued, characteristics which include the type of education (formal or non-formal) and the basic approach to teaching (knowledge-centred, curriculum-based learning or a pupil-centred approach based on his behaviour, aspirations and aptitudes); the learning climate and teacher-pupil relationship (strict or relaxed discipline, a hierarchical or free style of relations); the methods used (directed teaching or discovery learning), the resources available (especially audio-visual equipment), and the level of training and availability of teachers and other educational personnel. Activities should also be geared to the stage of development and level of instruction (primary education, 6-12 years old; lower secondary education, 12-15 years old; upper secondary and vocational training, 15-18 years old; post-secondary and higher education) and to the educational structure concerned (school, courses for adults, out-of-school activities, youth movements and church organizations, sports clubs, etc., and general lifelong education). Thus preventive action in education must be understood in context and applying systems analysis.[3]

Lastly, educational action designed for drug abuse prevention is rather different from other forms of teaching aimed at the mastery of a specific discipline in that its purpose is not simply to dispense information with a view to building up knowledge. We have realized for some time education seen as the dispensing, often without selection or prior study of the environment is not only ineffective but frequently counter-productive owing to the danger that an attraction will be engendered (curiosity, the forbidden fruit). In consequence, preventive education does not seek to convey new knowledge (have chemistry lessons on ethanol, ethyl alcohol, ever had a preventive effect?) but rather to prompt behavioural changes which frequently survive school days.

This role situates drug abuse prevention education among the multidisciplinary educational actions concerned with social problems involved with the quality of life, such as environmental education, population education, education in favour of health, nutrition and physical fitness, civic education and moral education. Such a diversity makes it virtually impossible to propose models, advocate a particular approach or predict the effectiveness of this or that activity. An activity's efficacity depends in fact on the educational context and the socio-cultural environment. There is no doubt that any activity out of tune with its surroundings is destined to be ineffective.

It is nevertheless worth drawing upon the rich and varied documentation collected by Unesco to attempt a reasoned typology of drug use education with the purpose of helping all those confronted with the problems of preventive education, irrespective of the level of decision involved (senior national or regional officials, curriculum development specialists, school heads or the people running associations, teachers, educators and parents) to compare their own experiences with those elsewhere in the international community.

Tables 1, 2 and 3 summarize the three dimensions of this typology: Table 1, the chosen educational strategy, or the educational approach; Table 2, target groups; and Table 3, type of activity and teaching materials.

These three dimensions interact; in other words, certain approaches are associated with target populations and certain types of activities or teaching aids are associated with particular target groups and approaches.

Three main approaches are distinguished in Table 1 to the implementation of preventive activities in education:

A direct substance-centred approach, in which various concepts related to the nature and use of drugs are taught directly in the classroom or during out-of-school educational activities. As the drugs concerned are legal substances, the aim is to encourage abstinence or self-control over consumption.

An alternative approach, which seeks to influence the immediate environment, assumes that drug abuse is a sign of maladjustment to the environment and society comparable to violence, vandalism and theft. This approach, with its non-emphasis on the actual drugs, aims at facilitating integration into the community by increasing participation in responsibilities and individual decision-taking and by proposing intellectual, social, cultural and recreational activities capable of replacing drugs.

It must be pointed out here that these two approaches are not selective: they are aimed rather at the whole of a given public, and they do not distinguish between users and non-users.

Table 1.   Three approaches to drugs and narcotic abuse prevention education

---

Direct drug-centred approaches
Educational action may utilize various channels:
Special courses
Education in health and hygiene
Moral, religious or civic education
Inclusion in courses in the humanities, the social sciences or exact sciences
Education related to the quality of life
Extra-curricular or out-of-school activities
Adult education activities

Approaches aimed at changing the immediate environment
The purpose of the educational action may be:
Improvement of school life
Supplementary activities in organized clubs
Reduction of the risk factors through organized leisure activities
Organization of socially useful activities
Promotion of social and professional integration by means of counselling and placement services

Indirect and selective approaches aimed at individuals
The educational action will concentrate on:
Stimulating the awareness of teaching staff, educators and youth leaders
Stimulating the awareness of parents
Providing counsellors for young persons or adults.

The third approach is indirect and selective: the educational action is individualized and conducted by adults, teachers, specialist educators, youth leaders or parents, and sometimes even by the opinion leaders of the group. It is based on the assumption that the vulnerable pupil or young person must be helped, and this calls for active co-operation between the various persons involved in the educational action, the school, the family and the community in particular.

These three approaches are not mutually exclusive but rather complement and reinforce one another; third approach in particular is a vital back-up for the other two.

To simplify matters, we have distinguished several ways and means of implementing each of these three approaches. The different possibilities are particularly significant in the case of a direct approach since they often reflect radically different methods of teaching.

The principal ways and means of implementing the direct approach are as follows:

A special course on the nature and effects of drugs.

Sensitization and scientific information about drugs included in the health, hygiene and nutrition curriculum.

Instruction on the effects of drug abuse in the curricula of moral, religious or civic education.

An 'incorporated' course, i.e. one that seeks to incorporate drug-related concepts by progressive, systematic and multi-disciplinary teaching in the context of various disciplines such as languages, literature, history, geography, chemistry, biology, the arts, etc.

A multidisciplinary course on the quality of life with the intention of creating positive attitudes to certain social problems such as the problems of population, the environment and drug use.

Extra-curricular and out-of-school activities, surveys and reports (visits to hospitals or centres that treat drug addicts), health clubs, health camps.

Information on the nature and effects of drugs provided during adult education activities (literacy courses, retraining courses, vocational training courses). The International Labour Organisation (ILO) supports many activities in this field, particularly as part of the struggle against alcoholism in industry.

For the second group of approaches, the following ways and means should be distinguished:

Improvement of school life: establishment of better relations between the pupils and the school's teaching and other staff, pupil involvement in decisions regarding the rules of the school, discipline and the choice of activities.

Organized clubs: astronomy, nature protection, computers, model-making, etc.

Reduction of risk factors: opening of youth clubs serving refreshments, organization of leisure activities (dancing, music, drama, arts, martial arts, scouting, excursions, travel, etc.).

Organization of socially useful activities in the school or community: tutoring classmates or younger pupils, helping the sick, the handicapped or the elderly, etc. The real purpose of such activities is to discourage behaviour which tends eventually to cut off people like drug addicts, handicapped persons or the elderly from society.

Educational and vocational guidance, holiday arrangements for younger persons.

Reducing risk factors and proposing activities to replace the consumption of drugs are a particularly important function of prevention programmes for young, high-risk persons in the cities, especially in rapidly expanding cities.

The indirect and selective approaches include such activities as:

Drawing the attention of teaching staff, educators and youth leaders to drug-related problems and improving interpersonal communication (group dynamics, training in listening and in conducting interviews, etc.). The World Health Organization (WHO) organizes such a course for health personnel, especially in developing countries.

Drawing the attention of parents to these problems and improving their ability to communicate with their children (parents' meetings, school for parents, parents' associations).

Providing counsellors (in the schools, in such associations or in the community) who have been specially trained to help maladjusted children, youths or adults.

Table 2 sets out the target groups of preventive education and calls for little comment. Apart from the division into age-groups, the reader will note distinctions that reflect the structure of the target audiences,

which determines the form of the messages addressed to each group. For example, the 'captive' and 'semi-captive' audiences in formal education and out-of-school activities are contrasted with the 'non-captive' audiences, which may be organized/structured (movements or associations) or non-organized/structure (radio listeners or television viewers). Any educational action aimed at a non-captive audience has to begin by attracting and then holding its attention.

Table 3 displays the types of teaching activities capable of furthering prevention and the teaching materials employed for both information campaigns and education in the strict sense. The difference between information materials and teaching materials lies in the self-sufficiency of the former (posters or leaflets, for example) whereas the latter represent a stage in the teaching process and imply preparation and follow-up. However, information materials can always be incorporated into a course of instruction.

The types of teaching activities set out in Table 3 are almost exclusively concerned with the direct approach, and are closely related to ways and means of implementing it. There are no teaching activities specific to preventive education in the alternative approach, which relies on active teaching methods. As for the indirect approaches, we possess little information and few case-studies on the actual activities and materials employed apart from a few examples of pamphlets and magazines aimed at alerting and informing.

Among the different types of teaching activities, it is important to emphasize the major role played by active methods-discovery learning, investigations, discussions and drama. Such activities, aimed at strengthening the independence of pupils and young persons and fostering self-expression and responsibility, are often based on teaching materials designed to provoke reactions or stimulate discussion, as in the case of multimedia materials, video cassettes and feature or documentary films.

Finally, certain teaching materials may be produced by the teachers in the school, though most are prepared by national institutions specializing in drug-use prevention and by international organizations.

Table 2. Target groups of drug and narcotics abuse prevention education

Formal education	Age-group	Out-of-school activities
Primary	6-12	Children
Lower secondary	12-15	Urban or rural teenagers
Upper secondary	15-18	
Post secondary	>18	Young adults
Teaching staff		Instructors and educators

Associations, movements and organizations
Youth movements
Professional associations
Confessional organizations
Sports clubs, cultural associations, etc.
Parents associations, women's movements

General public
Young people
Parents
Consumers
Radio listeners and television viewers
Readers of newspapers, magazines, etc.

Very rarely, such materials are developed by institutions or publishers responsible for drawing up and producing ordinary teaching materials used in the schools, such as textbooks and audiovisual materials.

All this goes to show that drug abuse prevention education remains an adjunct to curricula and out-of-school educational activities and hence an extra burden. In most cases, therefore, it requires special resources, especially financial, and is often left to institutions outside the control of educational authorities. This situation hampers the extension of drug-related education with the result that most of the activities and materials identified remain experimental and limited in scope. This is why Unesco is endeavouring to promote the gradual integration of preventive education into formal and non-formal education with a view to ensuring its general development and its financing through the regular education budget.

Whatever the approach, target group, activity or setting, the purpose of drug-related education is to contribute, through a sustained effort directed at the awareness, knowledge and behaviour of young people and adults, to reducing the demand for legal or illegal drugs.

It is a long and unceasing battle and its results are not easily assessable: the testing ot knowledge is but marginally useful and analyses of the reduction in demand, feasible only after a long period of efforts, rarely distinguish the role of education in the overall policy of prevention. This often makes it quite difficult to persuade the authorities, particularly the education authorities, to act in this field and free the necessary resources.

It has nevertheless been shown, as many involved in the struggle will bear out, that a lasting reduction in the demand for drugs cannot be achieved without practical educational work among young people and adults, concentrating on investigating and explaining both the underlying and the immediate causes of drug use, as well as helping young people and adults to solve their

Table 3. Drug abuse: preventive education
activities and materials

Types of activities

Lessons and lectures
Drawings, collages
Production of posters and leaflets
Observation and self-observation
Analysis of documents
Scientific experiments
Fieldwork
Discussions based on items in the news or
on audiovisual programmes
Play-acting and corporal expression
Group dynamics
Health camps

Form of materials

Information materials:
Slogans
Leaflets
Posters
Children's drawings
Pamphlets
Films and television programmes
Specialist magazines

Teaching materials:
Model lessons
Teacher guides
Exercise sheets
Information packages including basic facts,
instructions for the teacher and sources for
further information
Multimedia packages
Video cassettes
Films and television programmes
Songs

---

problems, make their decisions and lead their
lives without the need for drugs, and on
involving the community as a whole in
prevention activities.

The reasoned typology presented here is
illustrated by the panorama of preventive
education activities appended to this study.
The selection of actions, which have been
undertaken in a wide range of sociocultural
and economic contexts, testify to the immense
diversity of prevention-oriented approaches
and activities taking place throughout the
world.

NOTES

1. Nowlis, op. cit., p. 43.
2. Preventive education is a form of primary
   prevention that seeks to prevent the
   emergence of a disturbance, process or
   problem (see Chapter 1).
3. Unesco, *A Systems Approach to Teaching
   and Learning Procedures: A Guide for
   Educators.* 2nd rev. and exp. ed., Paris,
   Unesco, 1981.

12 THINGS TO DO INSTEAD OF SMOKING CIGARETTES.

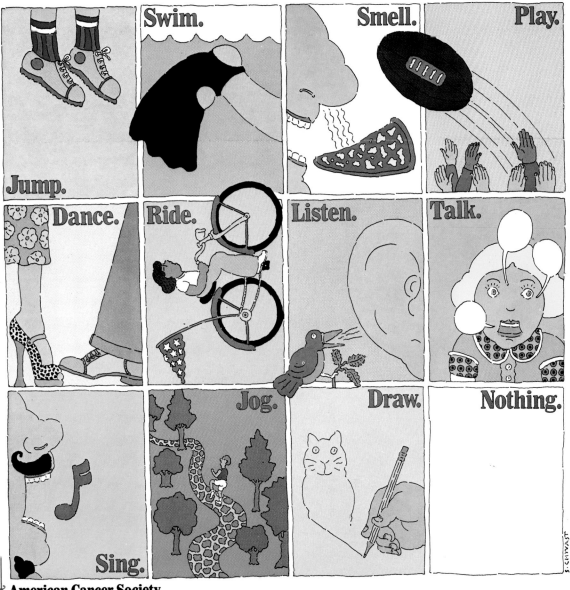

American Cancer Society

4. Evaluating preventive education

The last twenty years have seen great efforts to provide staff and finance for the fight against drug abuse as can be seen from the appended documents. Certain countries have launched ambitious anti-drug programmes involving treatment and repression as well as prevention.

Unfortunately, the design of many prevention-oriented programmes does not provide for an evaluation phase, thereby rendering impossible objective assessment of their results.

This omission also precludes comparison between programmes. It is a serious weakness, which many national and international bodies are trying to remedy. Admittedly, the evaluation of prevention work poses very thorny problems of methodology; over 100 articles, the majority in specialist journals, have been devoted to research on the subject. These studies generally attempt to measure the impact of a drug abuse prevention programme on the desire to consume drugs or on attitudes towards drugs. Most are focused on short campaigns in schools where the usual strategy is to provide information on the legal, physiological and psychological consequences of drug abuse. Other strategies rely on persuasion, psychological counselling, group dynamics or parental support. The most common method of evaluation is to ask the young people concerned to fill in a questionnaire immediately after the prevention campaign.

This questionnaire is sometimes followed up by a second evaluation a few months later with a view to obtaining a better picture of the medium-term effectiveness of the programme. The most rigorous studies compare the subsequent behaviour of a target group with that of another comparable group in the same community. This ensures that any changes observed may be attributed to the prevention work rather than to other factors concerning the population as a whole. Broadly speaking, prevention programmes produce a significant increase in knowledge about drugs and have a marginally favourable impact on attitudes. Certain studies have shown, however, that changes in permissive or non-permissive attitudes towards drugs on the part of young people or adults do not necessarily indicate behavioural changes or, more specifically, a reduction in drug consumption, hence the call for direct and indirect indicators to give a more accurate estimate of the extent to which the programmes achieve their goals.

We need a more precise definition of the objectives of prevention-oriented education. Is it intended, for example, to promote abstinence or simply to delay the onset of drug use in general or of certain particular drugs? Should preventive action deal with drug use or simply with drug abuse? Should it pay more particular attention to certain groups at risk? What strategy should be preferred, providing information or attempting to change the social or psychological factors which encourage the consumption of drugs?

The present trend is to devise evaluation models which serve as a framework for those in charge of prevention programmes. Three levels of evaluation can be distinguished:

Study of the prevention process, which takes into consideration the chosen target group, the teaching methods employed, the selection of prevention agents, etc.

Analysis of the results obtained, which shows whether the programme has had a significant effect on the participants and, if so, whether it has been positive.

Impact evaluation, which seeks to assess the general repercussions of the programme on the community as a whole. For this level, indicators such as the prevalence or extent of drug use, judicial statistics, or more specific epidemiological surveys are employed.

The prevention team will involve all those concerned by the programme (both helpers and participants) in the various evaluation procedures. The usual approach is to make use of self-evaluation techniques, more or less formal interviews, texts or questionnaires. Only through constant feedback from the participants in the programme can the work of prevention be satisfactorily adjusted as a function of its effects.

The final analysis of the results usually leads the organizers of a prevention programme to redefine objectives and means to increase effectiveness of subsequent actions. Certain setbacks prove to be beneficial since they compel re-evaluation of the theories explicitly, or more often implicitly, underlying the preventive actions. For example, certain prevention policies do not pay enough atention to socio-cultural context while others minimize personality factors and underestimate the degree of maladjustment of 'high-risk' young people.

The complexity of drug dependence makes it essential to co-ordinate action taken by the various sectors of the society (health, schooling, employment) at the regional or national level. It has also become clear that information on the achievements of the most advanced countries in this field does not circulate well. Indeed, the main purpose of this book is to facilitate the flow of information.

THE FUTURE

First, an observation: several new methods of preventive education, unknown a few years ago, are at present being tried out. Advances in such fields as developmental psychology, psychology and epidemiology are making a major contribution to the renewal of theory. Our understanding of the influence of friends, the family and the various social environments on the behaviour of drug users is steadily improving.

Since so many participating adolescents are subsequently lost track of, it is difficult for follow-up studies to gauge the stability of the behaviour changes brought about. Current research in methodology is trying to overcome some of the obstacles.

The relative uncertainty regarding the validity of self-evaluations carried out by young people in the course of surveys is a problem difficult to avoid. In many cases, the smallness of the sample makes it unwise to draw general conclusions from the results. Too few studies are focused on poverty-stricken or fringe groups of young people even though the urgent need for vigorous presention work in favour of such disadvantaged groups is well known.

The results achieved in recent years are making it possible for preventive education organizations to take increasingly specific action geared to the individual characteristics of the high-risk groups concerned. Current pedagogical research is also encouraging a wider range of prevention strategies, which will eventually strengthen the relative role of preventive education among means of combating drug abuse. Through facilitating the exchange of information and experience in this field, international co-operation has already proved beneficial. International organizations still have an important role to play in fostering the implementation of prevention strategies commensurate with the scale of the problem.

Annexes: Examples of prevention work

In most countries there are three main approaches to prevention work against the use of legal or illegal drugs:

The direct approach, centred on the substances and aimed at both users and non-users.

The alternative approach, directed at action on the environment; it is focused not so much on the drugs themselves as on the social integration of individuals.

The indirect and selective approach, centred on the individual and directed at sharpening the awareness of prevention agents (educators, parents, counsellors, community leaders).

The following pages illustrate these three approaches in action in different countries and offer some examples of how such preventive activities may be evaluated. This selection cannot, of course, cover every type of educational activity and its evaluation, every geographical region or every drug consumed, but the cases presented give a fairly accurate picture of the various approaches discussed in this book and thus provide a basis for reflection on future actions.

The majority of the documents concerned have been summarized but the accompanying references will enable the interested reader to obtain the full texts.

I. The direct approach

Facts and feelings about drugs but decisions about situations;
Teachers manual: a drug education manual outlining a short course
for use in secondary schools, 1982*

This manual defines working with particular situations, starting from the hypothesis that the
use of drugs is principally determined by opportunity. What are offer situations and how
should one react? This is the situational approach.
Teaching objective: to be more lucid and more determined in a choice situation.
Group work.

MODEST AIMS OF THE SITUATIONAL APPROACH

These methods have been designed with particular educational aims in mind. The two overall aims are:

Increased knowledge about legal and illegal drugs, of their effects at the time taken, and of the effects of long-term patterns of use.

Enhanced decision-making skills, defined here as the ability to anticipate and discuss the 'choice-situations' in which teenagers may find they have access to a drug for the first time; and ability to apply knowledge to such situations.

Much more ambitious aims, such as prevention of drug experimentation, minimizing the proportion of experimenters who go on to develop heavy involvement with legal or illegal drugs or reducing some other aspects of drug-related harm, may or may not be realistic even considering them, health education may be 'trying to run before it can walk'.

Situational education aims to fulfil limited, preparatory aims, specifically to increase pupils' knowledge and to enhance their decision-making skills. These methods will be most appealing to those teachers who are fortunate enough to teach in a school which has not been panicked into taking an educationally unsound, 'fire-brigade' response to drugs.

UNIT 2: DECISIONS ABOUT 'OFFER-SITUATIONS'

Basic ideas presented in this unit

There are many theories about why people take legal and illegal drugs. Being offered a drug is an important reason. Most people believe that they would not take an

---

* Published by the Institute for the Study of Drug Dependence (ISDD), 1-4 Hatton Place, Hatton Garden, London EC1N 8ND, United Kingdom.

illegal drug, but most of them have not been offered one.

As pupils go through their teens, it becomes more likely that they will be offered a drug that they have not been offered before.

Most offers come from somebody about their own age (not from an adult 'pusher'), and are made in a friendly social situation.

So, if people want to have a sensible discussion about whether or not they would take a drug, they have to imagine what it would be like to be offered it.

Different people will find themselves in different situations and will value things differently and so will make different choices.

The manual begins by describing the preparation by the teacher. The course then takes the form of group work, with the teacher's questions provoking a discussion and keeping it going.

Ask pupils: Why do some people take drugs, and some not?

Allow free response, and then build upon pupils' ideas to include the possibilities outlined in the following paragraphs.

There are all kinds of theories about why people start taking drugs and *none* of them have been proved: the 'weak personality' theory, the 'evil pusher' theory, the 'pleasure' theory, the 'rebel' theory, the 'curiosity' theory, the 'doesn't know any better' theory, the 'fashion' theory, and the 'in-with-the-crowd' theory.

Sometimes people might take a legal or illegal drug just because it is offered to them, the 'because-it-is-offered' theory.

Are you likely to be offered legal or illegal drugs?

What is it like to be offered drugs?

Comparing offers refused with offers accepted (e.g. cigarettes; alcohol) in one choice-situation, sometimes say 'no thanks' to the same drug in a different situation.

Looking to the future - possible offer-situations

This situational role-play can be followed by a Panel Session, during which selected pupils comment on the situation just acted out. Following this, an examination can be carried out into situations in which illicit drugs may be offered and the probability of these situations coming up. The exercises will help predict the situations. Posters.

Drugs and other people

You can't please everybody: Make one list of people who would think it all right if you took the drug, and another list of people who would think less of you if they knew that you had taken it.

How to respond in situations in which *other people's* use of drugs is in question.

Work should deal with possible situations, using class discussion, role-play, etc

Option - Minimizing harm. This option may be worthwhile if pupils show signs of concern over their own/friends use of legal or illegal drugs, and seek ways of minimizing the chances of coming to harm. Continue group work, using questions, answers, class discussion on:

■ Reducing chances of getting into a habit

■ Reducing medical harm and unpleasant experiences. Consider how to get the best effect from a legal or illegal drug and how to get the worst effect from a legal or illegal drug.

■ Reducing legal harm and harmful 'images' as a drug-taker (boozer, glue-sniffer).

Option - If you were a politician. People sometimes say that 'something ought to be done'. What would you do? List things that some people say ought to be done and difficulties encountered:

■ heavier fines and prison sentences,

■ a ban on all cigarette advertising,

■ making it legal to use cannabis (like cigarettes and alcohol),

■ a complete ban on the sale of cigarettes, etc.

Closing topic - If you were the teacher. Would you teach about legal or illegal drugs if you were the teacher? If so, what would you say? This work could involve an essay illustrated with posters/collages.

MAKING DECISIONS ABOUT DRUG EDUCATION: CONSIDER THE CURRICULUM CONTEXT

No teaching approach can be appraised purely 'on its own merits', without regard to the situation (characteristics of school, pupils, development of curricula, teachers' particular skills, etc.) in which it would be applied.

Here are aspects of the whole situation in schools that are relevant to decisions about drug education:

The likelihood of pupils encountering choice-situations

Teachers will have to make their own estimations of the situation obtaining in their school.

Other professionals, such as youth workers, social workers or police, may be able to supply 'guesstimates' of pupils' likely contact with drugs - legal or illegal.

Some practitioners' experiences lead them to identify use of particular legal/illegal drugs and attitudes with particular social class and ethnic groups.

The school's response to discovery of drug experimentation

Teachers' legal obligations under the law are the same as those of any other citizen. There is no legal obligation to pass on information about a pupil's drug use to the police. It is not illegal for a pupil to possess or drink alcohol. Nor is glue or solvent-sniffing illegal. It is illegal to sell alcohol to somebody under 18 years of age. However, the sale of alcohol to people under 18 is common.

If the police are informed about illegal drug use amongst pupils, then they may or may not proceed with a full investigation, and may or may not prosecute. Fewer schools probably call the police in than they used to a few years ago, and the police are probably less keen to undertake this role than previously.

Some styles of response, for example, panic responses involving a heavy police presence in the school, are not compatible with the situational approach. Broadly speaking, it has been observed that a police-oriented response to pupils' drug experimentation coming to adult notice is more compatible with one-off 'warnings of danger' approaches involving outside lecturers or scare-films, than with the lower key, situational teaching.

The assumption that experimentation with drugs is necessarily a symptom of psychological or emotional problems is incompatible with a situational approach which therefore cannot be used where these problems exist.

The 'soft curriculum'

The third aspect of the total situation in the school that is relevant to teachers' decisions about drug and alcohol education is the extent to which the 'soft curriculum' - health, social, moral and 'lifeskills' education - is developed in the school.

In some schools the soft curriculum is relatively poorly developed, and 'topics' are dealt with in 'one-offs', as urgent problems arise. They may not want to use these situational materials, since the topic approach is most generally associated with early panic phases of response and the situational approach may be found too 'low key' and lacking in urgency. At the other extreme, the minority of schools that have consolidated a truly integrated curriculum in health-related or social education may also find the situational approach inapplicable as it stands.

Most schools will fall in between these two extremes - curriculum integration neither absent, nor total; it is in such schools that the question of whether to adopt a situational approach to drug education is most likely to arise.

This approach has been shown to do no discernible evil. It's suitability in particular schools will, however, depend not just on the teachers' appraisals of its strengths and weaknesses but also on the school context.

The Hexagonal Kite*

Health education booklet: special course on tobacco. A study of the harm done by tobacco, carried out by means of group games, the water bottle experiment, advertisements cut out from magazines and a critical analysis.

The booklet contains an illustration of a group of six children, of whom one, Riton, is smoking. They are in a rowing boat. Riton falls in the water and, as he is short of breath, he nearly drowns. His friends advise him to stop smoking, but Riton replies 'I don't know of anything to do that's cheaper than smoking.'

Back in the classroom, three questions are asked:

Is tobacco harmful to health?

Is it true, as the advertisements imply, that smokers are always healthy, lucky, happy people?

Could people buy other, more attractive things with the money they spend on tobacco?

The following experiment will help us to understand exactly what tobacco is:

Wash a transparent plastic bottle and fill it almost entirely with water.

Plug up the neck of the bottle with cotton-wool.

Make a hole in the teat of a feeding bottle so that you can place a cigarette in the hole, leaving the end which will be lighted projecting from the teat. Then seal the bottle as hermetically as possible with the teat, the edges of which can, if necessary, be sealed to the neck of the bottle with wax or similar material.

Pierce a hole in the lower part of the bottle with a needle, light the cigarette and leave it to burn away.

This experiment can be carried out and commented on in class. The pupils can then be questioned on what they can see and on the relation between the experiment and what happens when one smokes. Next, they are asked to draw a sketch of Riton's body, showing the principal organs which enable him to take part in sports, to eat, or simply to enjoy life. They are asked to describe organs vital to life and to paint in grey on the sketch those which are affected by tobacco - lungs, heart, stomach, brain, arteries and veins.

WHAT ADVERTISEMENTS DESCRIBE

Is it true that smokers are as healthy and as much as ease as the advertisements imply?

The children are asked to cut out all the cigarette advertisements they can find in magazines at home and then to classify them according as they refer to sports, social life, or people who are well known or popular. They study these examples and consider whether such advertisements are honest.

To find the answer to this question, it is suggested that the children carry out a survey among their acquaintances so as to arrive at the truth, using the following questionnaire:

Do you think that smoking makes one feel happier?

Have you already tried to give up smoking?

Is it difficult to give up smoking permanently?

The children study the questionnaires that have been filled in, and are asked to consider whether the advertisements are honest and whether smokers are more or less free than those who do not smoke.

They now have the following evidence:

The bottle that smokes.

The sketch of Riton's body with the organs affected by the action of tobacco.

---

* Ramón Mendoza and Teresa Salvador, 'La cometa de seis puntas', Barcelona, Barcanova, 1983, 64 pp. (Cuadernos de educación sanitaria).

Cigarette advertisements cut out of magazines.

Three tables showing the replies to the questionnaire.

'You now know more about tobacco. Using all this information, draw a poster illustrating what you know about smoking and the aspect of smoking that you think should be most emphasized.

'Here are three examples of such posters. Look at them carefully and think about how you will do your own.'

With the money people spend on tobacco, what could they buy that is more attractive?

How much could they save in a week, a month or a year?

It is suggested that an exhibition should be held at the school, showing the various items that the children have before them.

*Material for teaching about smoking**

This material is intended for teachers of pupils in the lower secondary school, for use in lessons on morals or civics in Gabon. It consists of: an example of a school record card for the first year of secondary school; and an example of a critical study of advertising for Marlboro cigarettes.

A RECENT PHENOMENON: TWO CONCOMITANT FACTS

There has been a general improvement in the standard of living over the last forty years and particularly the last thirty years.

At the same time, tobacco consumption has increased considerably.

New consumers: women, even before 1940 in the United States; since 1950 in Western Europe; more recently, young women (under 20).

The individual consumption of cigarettes has quadrupled in France in forty years, and there has been a similar increase in all countries where statistics are available. The same thing has happened in Third World countries since independence.

There has been a 'rapid, mortal and spectacular' increase in bronchial cancer, which has become the principal killer in modern cancerology.

The last American demographic report shows that in the twenty years from 1950 to 1970 mortality due to lung cancer, bronchitis, emphysema and asthma has doubled.

In the United States, deaths due to lung cancer have increased fivefold in women since 1958. The increase is so great that it will be the principal cause of death from cancer by 1983, its incidence and gravity overtaking breast cancer, which was, up to then, the leading cause of death from cancer in women.

As early as 1950, doctors were pointing out the link between the consumption of tobacco and cancer of the respiratory tract. Studies on tobacco smoke have shown that tobacco contains powerful carcinogens, and that even in minute quantities it can start the malignant process, particularly if there is a predisposition to cancer.

This last point provides an answer to smokers who pin their hopes on cigarettes with a lower level of toxicity which have been manufactured since the danger was first observed.

MISINFORMATION BY THE TOBACCO INDUSTRY, WHOSE ONE AIM IS TO SELL TOBACCO

Harmless cigarettes. Relying on the fact that it is possible to manufacture less toxic cigarettes as is now the practice, for example by using a more porous paper, thus causing more rapid combustion and therefore a reduction in the concentration of tar, and by making more efficient filters, the tobacco manufacturers boost cigarettes which they say are 'harmless'.

They are lying. Tobacco smoke is dangerous no matter how it is absorbed and filtered. It is even dangerous for those who breathe it without smoking themselves.

Some figures. Statistics from the Curie Institute of Cancerology in Paris, taken from a survey made over a period of three years. Of 1,600 patients with cancer of the larynx, 98 per cent were found to be smokers. This is a particularly mutilating form of cancer; it entails the removal of the larynx, the organ that produces sound, and it results in the loss of the voice; re-education then becomes necessary in order to obtain an 'oesophageal' voice.

---

* Extracts from the working paper of the Gabonese Delegation to the 'Workshop for the Production of Material for Use in Education on Problems linked to Drug Usage', organized by Unesco at Abidjan, Côte d'Ivoire, 18-27 July 1979.

The Moscow Congress held in 1968 declared that tobacco was the prime cause of bronchial and lung cancer.

A *survey* carried out in the United Kingdom in 1971 revealed that 38,000 men and 4,000 women, a total of 42,000 people, i.e. roughly the equivalent of the population of Port Gentil, die prematurely each year in England and Wales because of tobacco smoking.

To smoke tobacco is dangerous - that is the inevitable conclusion.

It therefore seems desirable that young people should be informed of the damage to the body caused by the use of tobacco, so that they can be protected from it.

The more one smokes, the greater the danger
Other circumstances being the same, cancer of the respiratory tracts is more common and the mortality rate is higher among smokers than among non-smokers, and these figures rise according to the amount of tobacco smoked daily.

SCHOOL RECORD CARD

First year of secondary school

The teacher should give a talk on the damage caused by the use of tobacco, and then the pupils should discuss what has been said.

REMARKS ON THE TALK

The first two points in the talk should be stressed, so as to get the pupils to reason about the subject. They are:

Step 1. We note that four times as many cigarettes were smoked in 1980 as in 1940; and at the same time there is a proliferation of cancer of the respiratory tract.
Reasoning: Is there a connection between these two facts?
Hypothesis: Yes
The pupils must be shown the reasoning behind this.
Step 2. It must be proved that these two facts are connected.
How can that be done?

The pupils must be shown how research is carried out.
The patients are questioned (in 1,600 of cases of cancer of the larynx, 98 per cent were smokers).
Various experiments are performed on tobacco.
Analyses are made using modern technological methods.

Step 3. The conclusion is that tobacco is harmful because the hypothesis has been shown to be true.
Damage is done by tobacco to the respiratory tract; to the digestive tract; to the circulatory system; and to the nervous system.

Step 4. In order to save people from sickness, they must be informed.
That is why we tell school children about the harm done by tobacco. Sweden has decided to bring up the new generation to be non-smokers, and in the last few years nursery-school children have been taught about the dangers of tobacco. Parents play their part in their children's education.

REMARKS ON THE DISCUSSION

Aim: to induce the pupil to reason as follows:

- *I know* that tobacco can cause cancer, especially cancer of the larynx, which leads to terrible mutilation.
- *I know* that tobacco weakens the body.
- *I want* to remain strong and in good health. Who would deliberately choose to make himself ill?
- *I shall not smoke.*

Attemps to find reasons for smoking
Some pupils might say:
- others smoke;
- smoking looks smart, grown-up, or strong;
- smoking is pleasant.
Refutation: to imitate others, to do as 'the others' do, is not sensible. Acting like sheep is not being strong.
'The others' have not understood the truth, that smoking harms the whole body.

'Smoking is pleasant' is a misleading statement: a passing feeling of excitement is followed by a period of depression. This is true of any kind of excitement. (N.B. The teacher expresses the idea, but the way in which he does so must be adapted to the pupil's stage of development).

You smoke, and you are happy for a little while. Soon you feel sad. Then you smoke another cigarette to be cheerful again. That is how you become a smoker and harm your own body.

TEACHER'S SUGGESTION

Smoking is expensive. Make the pupils work out the annual tobacco budget of a smoker who smokes two packets a day. Instead of buying cigarettes, lighters, ashtrays, etc., it would be better to buy books and records.

ARGUMENTS THAT PUPILS MAY PUT FORWARD TO JUSTIFY SMOKING

A pupil might say: 'You can smoke without getting cancer', or 'Why not smoke just a little?'
Refutation: Once you start smoking, you start a process which you cannot stop, because nicotine is habit-forming. Heavy smokers who wish to break themselves of the habit have to be treated in hospitals. If they don't, they are in danger.
The sooner you start smoking, the sooner you experience a need to smoke. (Cf. note above)

ANOTHER ARGUMENT A PUPIL MAY PUT FORWARD

Pupil's argument: Mr . . . . (a teacher) smokes.
Reply: If Mr . . . . wishes to ruin his health, there is no reason why you should do so. Furthermore, tobacco does more harm to a child than to an adult. You should safeguard your health, which is the most important possession you have and the main requirement for happiness. To smoke, even a little, damages people's health, particularly that of a child.

Pupil's argument: My father smokes and he has not got cancer.
Reply: You should try to persuade your father to stop smoking, by reducing the number of cigarettes he smokes each day. That would be good for him and for you.
Pupil's argument: Cigarettes are advertised.
Reply: Industry and trade have only one goal - to sell. The salesman does not worry about your health. Your health is your own problem. You owe it to yourself to protect your health by not smoking.
The pupils should be asked to write in their notebooks what has struck them most in this discussion.

MATERIAL FOR A CRITICAL STUDY

It should be easy to obtain copies of this and other material in colour.

Critical study of advertising for Marlboro cigarettes

Description. Galloping across a stretch of water, a cowboy is about to catch a wild horse.

The trademark 'Marlboro' stands out in large white letters against a very dark sky.

At the bottom of the page, on the right, against a background of water and shingle, two packets of cigarettes are shown, one closed, the other open; the second is full, and two cigarettes are partly pulled out. Beside the packets are the words 'Marlboro, the world's number one selling cigarette'.

The question is: What is the *connection* between the scene and the cigarettes?
There is no apparent connection.
What *impression* does the scene make?
Action, strength, vigour (the cowboy's movements; the horses galloping; the water splashing).
The sight of a different world (the world of cowboys).
The *suggestion* that the advertisement is intended to make - the 'hidden meaning'.
Association between 'Marlboro' cigarettes and vigour.
Association between the cigarettes and a different world.

This is the principal aim of advertising.

Effect produced. Anyone who looks at the scene and is absorbed by the picture and thinks it attractive unconsciously allows the suggested association to make an impression on him. From there it is but a step to action: he gets some cigarettes, that is to say, he buys them.

Criticism. The scene is pleasant, but as the connection between strength, vigour, action and the act of smoking is a false one, comparing tobacco and vitamin C, the most elementary reasoning should stop one from falling into the trap laid by the advertisement.

Conclusion. One must find out the hidden meaning and think about it before coming to a decision.

Health careers. Teachers manual*

*Thirteen lesson-guides on health careers intended for teachers and youth workers (all drugs).
In what situations are drugs taken?
Emphasis is placed on leisure time most conducive to taking drugs.
Two lessons are presented in résumé here: the first deals with images of health and the quality
    of life, the second with drugs and use-situations (time-off).*

INTRODUCTION

This manual is intended for teachers of school-leavers (especially boys and girls in working class areas for whom conventional approaches to health and social education seem unsuitable), for youth workers, and for teachers in unemployment and training schemes in colleges of further education and community projects. It can be used over any period from a one-week intensive project to a year-long school-leaving course. Pupils are active collaborators in the course. Posed in quite general terms, the *course objectives* (as distinct from the objectives of any specific unit) are that the course facilitates pupils' ability to:

Understand that health is affected by work and living conditions or by responses (i.e. cultures, leisure patterns) to these;

Gain knowledge of some work and living conditions in the locality, and of some consequences for the health of local people.

Appraise their own current work and living conditions and health consequences.

Review their current responses (cultures, leisure habits) to these current and foreseeable conditions in the light of health consequences.

Suggest improvements for self and others.

Taken as a set, these course objectives contribute to the general aim of the course, to broaden pupils' conception of 'health' to include the health consequences of their present and foreseeable work and living conditions and of their responses to these conditions (in summary, to help pupils develop a rounded conception of their 'health careers'); and to give them opportunities to explore possible improvements in their health careers.

UNIT 1: IMAGES OF HEALTH

Preparation and resources:
- Newspapers, comics and magazines for cutting up.
- Plain white card to make 'flashcards'.
- Stiff cardboard, scissors, string.
- Access to a large scrapbook, or pin-boards.
- Copies of the time-spending questionnaire.

Ask pupils: What is health? Children's ideas of health generally revolve around the idea of *not being ill.* Encourage a more positive definition of health, e.g. feeling good, being happy, social competence.

Images of health and illness in the media: exercise

Distribute copies of daily newspapers, magazines, teenage comics to class and ask pupils to cut out all stories and all pictures that refer to physical, mental or social health in any way and comment on them, particularly those relevant to their own feelings.

Lead the discussion towards pupils' feelings about 'wellbeing' and health in their future lives.

Say to class: A time-spending disc, made in class, will be used, in conjunction with a time-spending questionnaire, by the pupils to discuss with friends, parents and other adults how they spend their time. Each pupil will carry out an interview survey out of school and then work in class on the results to

---

* Published by the Institute for the Study of Drug Dependence (ISDD), 1-4 Hatton Place, Hatton Garden, London EC1N 8ND, United Kingdom.

demonstrate the differences which emerge, depending on age or sex. In particular, everyone's health career will emerge.

After pupils have carried out their interviews, these are then discussed in the next available lesson. Discussion is best introduced by the teacher going round the class and asking each pupil who he or she interviewed. The teacher should be able to draw out some conclusions, e.g. contrasts between the sexes, contrasts between people who have different types of job and contrasts between those at different life stages.

The contrasts should bring out how different people spend their time; how they like that way of spending their time (does it make them feel well?); and how they got into such health careers.

Pupils should pin their questionnaires and any other relevant material on to the open file, on pinboards or in scrapbooks.

Introduce 'health career' idea: Explain that your health career is everything that you do that affects your health, happiness and general 'wellbeing'. The course is going to look at your health careers from now, up to your parents' age. The ways in which you spend your time determine your health, through work hazards, pollution, eating habits, patterns of use of alcohol and other drugs, that are typical of the occupational group, etc.

Ask class: What sort of 'health career' do the pupils think that they will have over the next few years?

UNIT 3: TAKING TIME OFF
MEDICINES, DRUGS AND HEALTH

Introduction: drugs and 'time off'

The teacher should ask pupils to examine the pictures, adverts and press headlines which concern themselves with legal and illegal drugs.

Point out to class that some are legal for all ages (e.g. coffee, tea); some are legal for adults (e.g. drinking in pubs); some are legal from the doctor (e.g. antibiotics, antidepressants); and some are illegal in all circumstances (e.g. cannabis, some other illegal drugs). Note also that some are more dangerous than others. (Relative dangers are dealt with later in the unit.) Now, *forgetting differences* between the different drugs, ignoring their differing effects and differing legal statuses, direct attention to their circumstances of use.

Question to class: How are each of the drugs used? At what time, in what sorts of situations? And what is the common element in the situation of use? Try to draw out the common aspect of use of drugs in periods of having 'time-off' from work. Examples:

Coffee, tea, cigarettes - used in breaks in the day.

Alcohol (and, less commonly, cannabis) - used at the end of the work-day, or at the end of the week.

Drugs from doctor - used in periods of illness, i.e. when not working, or working badly.

The common element in media portrayals of drug-use situations is the idea of 'time-off' from the work-day. 'Time-off' can be momentary, a ten-minute break, can occur during lunch or at the end of the day, or it can be an extended period of non-work.

Encourage pupils to say what period of 'time-off' is implied in each portrayal of drug use. This can be done verbally, or the various portrayals can be categorized and arranged on pinboards or cards under the headings:

A few moments or minutes off work (e.g. cigarette, coffee use at work, including during housework).

A few hours off, or the rest of the day off (e.g. drinking in the pub).

A few days or weeks off work (e.g. ill people taking medicine).

Reiterate: the common element is 'time off' work. Drug use is a 'holiday' from work, and the length of the 'holiday' varies from a few minutes to a few years.

Refer to 'time spending' questionnaires

The questionnaires on how local occupational groups spend time contains information about how they use legal drugs and so make a period of 'time off' for themselves. Refer pupils to these questionnaires, or refer to them yourself, pointing out that several hours

Factsheet on Drug Use in Working Life

How is it used?	What does it look like?	How is it taken?	Effects of occasional use?	Effects of repeated use?	Is it legal?
"Time for a fag" Taking a moment off and lighting a cigarette	Cigarettes	Smoked. Regular smokers find cigarettes relaxing and sometimes stimulating. Can delay hunger. Lasts 10–30 minutes.	Affects many parts of the body. Speeds up heart rate and increases blood pressure.	Possible damage to lungs and other parts of the body. Causes cancer. The body can begin to depend on nicotine	Legal to smoke cigarettes at any age Legal to buy them over 16.
"Time for a Coffee Break"	Coffee	Swallowed as a drink. Makes people more awake. Lasts several hours.	Helps concentration for a short while. Very large amount may kill.	Can be difficult to concentrate or sleep. Can be difficult to give up.	Legal for anybody to have, use or sell coffee.
"Getting through the day" Drugs taken to keep working	Aspirin	Swallowed as pills, powders or liquids. Stops pains and headaches. Lasts several hours.	Large amount can kill. Stomach bleeding possible even with small amounts.	Possible stomach damage	Legal for anybody to have or sell aspirin.
	Tranquillisers (eg. valium, librium)	Swallowed as pills. Lasts several hours.	Makes you more relaxed. Also drowsy. Large amounts kill if taken with alcohol.	Can make you more anxious. Difficult to give up.	Anyone can have and use tranquillisers but only a doctor can prescribe them.
"Let's meet after work"	Alcohol	Swallowed as a drink. Small amount makes people relaxed, large amount makes them 'drunk'. Lasts several hours.	Makes concentration and quick reactions difficult. Large amount can kill.	Possible damage to heart, liver, stomach, brain. Can become addictive and then withdrawal is difficult.	Illegal to sell alcohol without a licence. Legal to buy alcohol if aged over 18. Legal to drink in pub if over 18.
	Cannabis (pot, dope, hash, grass)	Smoked in a "joint" or pipe, by itself or with tobacco. Makes colours and sounds brighter and louder. Lasts 20 minutes to several hours.	Makes concentration and quick reactions difficult	Possible lung damage, especially if smoked with tobacco.	Illegal to have or sell.
"I'm off work today" Drug use as a sign of illness.	Other drugs and medicine from the Doctor.	Taken as directed by Doctor	(Ask your Doctor)	(Ask your Doctor)	Legal to have any medicine prescribed by Doctor.

For use with Unit 3 of *Health Careers,* ISDD, London.

a week are spent using legal drugs to make periods of time off. Approximately how many hours? Which drugs are used?

If the pupils enter these occupations, are they likely to develop similar patterns of legal drug use?

'My chemical career'

Because every type of job career seems to involve a 'chemical career' of taking a variety of drugs in 'time off' periods, most pupils can work out their own likely 'chemical career'. For instance, in the first ten years, age group 16 to 25, how many cups of coffee, how many cigarettes, how many alcoholic drinks will they consume?

Conclusion

We can't understand drug use without understanding 'time off', understanding pupil's work-situation. Pupils could conclude the unit by designing health education materials that show how their own and others' chemical careers are connected with local occupations and cultures - or could suggest ideas for such designs, to be taken up in the final unit.

*Healthy lifestyle camps. An alternative approach to drug education, health camp Luther Heights, 1980**

Recounts the experience of a health camp in Australia.
Aims: to develop a good self-image and communicate well with others by developing an independence and becoming aware of what constitutes health.
A positive behavioural conception of health.

Health camps have been conducted in Australia since 1970: the aims, objectives and format of the camps have altered considerably as research into drug education as a preventive strategy has evolved from a drug-oriented information-based approach to one of a behaviour-oriented positive health approach.[1]

The camps are conducted over the period of a weekend.

The aims and objectives are to effect behaviour change in:

■ Trainee teachers as group leaders.
■ Grade 11 high school students (self-selected from various Queensland high schools).

This report pertains to the Health Camp held from 7 to 9 November 1980 at Luther Heights Camp, Coolum Beach, Sunshine Coast. Fifteen trainee teachers attended as leaders, and fifty students participated.

GETTING TO KNOW EACH OTHER

Considerable time is spent in providing structured activities which will facilitate the development of self-awareness, and communication skills which enable participants to get to know each other while enhancing self-concept.

During the early stages of the camp, emphasis is placed on the development of a strong sense of co-operation, group cohesion and mutual acceptance while recognizing the uniqueness and value of each individual within the group.

INFORMAL TIME

Free time is a valuable opportunity for camp leaders to demonstrate that they recognize the maturity of the students to behave responsibly, and to model the values of trust. This is the time when students can put into practice the skills they have thus far learned, and can begin to question and process the camp experience. Informal time refers to a wide variety of activities, such as beach walks and swims, etc.

During these times, the various camp participants choose to participate at their own desired level. As a general rule, these times are scheduled as a relaxation period before meals.

PERSONAL HEALTH RECORD

Students spend up to three hours learning about the parameters of physical health by actually assessing their own personal health status. Working in groups allows them to be able to compare their health status with others (as a learning tool, not competitively) and thereby learn to recognize individual variations.

Students are encouraged to compare these objective measures with subjective estimations of well-being and wellness; and thus arrive at a conclusion about health as a total lifestyle process, for which they, as individuals, are largely responsible.

The response to this section has invariably involved enthusiasm and insight on the part of the students.

---

* Prepared by the Division of Health Promotion, Queensland Department of Health, Australia.

SELF-AWARENESS AND SELF-CONCEPT

Studies by Nowlis[2] suggest the important role which low self-esteem plays in deviant behaviours and drug abuse.

A preventive education approach aims at enhancing self-concept and increasing skills in human relations and communication. Many of these activities are informal and unstructured. More structured activities are offered as formal learning experiences. Students report that they find these sessions tremendously stimulating and useful.

RELAXATION AND STRESS MANAGEMENT

Before retiring each night, students are invited to experience a conscious relaxation method/training session. Usually students experience deep muscle relaxation and guided imagery. After the experience students informally discuss the experience and practical issues regarding stress management. Depending on the need and response of the group, the topic may be further expanded to include time management, assertiveness training and interpersonal communication.

RECREATION OPTIONS

Current trends in preventive drug education promote creative and constructive use of leisure time as alternatives to self-destructive behaviours such as drug use. Saturday afternoon is devoted to the provision of a wide variety of 'leisure options' including bushwalks, archery, square dancing, craft, drama, kite making and flying, tennis, etc.

These options are based on principles of co-operation and self-expression in preference to any competitiveness.

SATURDAY EVENING

Students are encouraged to use Saturday evening imaginatively, and then suggestions are taken up: a form of fancy-dress dance, supper, sometimes as a campfire and sing-song, followed by some form of relaxation experience.

MEALS

Meals are categorized as an activity because of their relation to the principles of modelling desirable behaviours and experiential learning.

NOTES

1. H. Nowlis, *Drugs Demystified: Drug Education,* 3rd ed., Paris, Unesco, 1982.
2. H. Nowlis, *Prevention is Not Easy*, p. 16, National Information Service on Drug Abuse, May 1980, (Technical Information Bulletin, No. 62).

*In the name of God, the merciful, the compassionate**

Lessons on the consumption of alcohol (second year class at the Mabrouka Institute, which is attached to the Bakht er-Ruda Pedagogical Institute, Sudan).
The lessons are based on the precepts of the Koran, and the aim is to make the pupils realize the harm caused by the consumption of alcohol and to develop their sense of responsibility.

FIRST AND SECOND LESSONS

The first two lessons are entitled 'The foundations of stability' and relate to verses from the Koran which are found in the second-year manual of the Mabrouka Institute.

First verse: 'Yes, God commands equity, charity and generosity towards close relations. He forbids depravity, reprehensible acts and oppression. He encourages you. Perhaps you will reflect on this.'

Second verse: 'Wine, games of chance, dolmens and divining arrows are an abomination and a work of the devil. Avoid them . . . perhaps you will be happy'.

First lesson

Aims:

To develop the pupil's sense of responsibility for his health and to encourage discipline in social behaviour;

To turn the pupil's mind away from things that harm him and make him unable to reason about himself and the people around him.

Steps in the first lesson:
Guidance on different kinds of depravity and reprehensible acts and the bad effects they have on society, health and the economy.

The teacher should state what are the many different kinds of depravity and reprehensible acts. They include the consumption of alcohol and, more generally, all drugs, whether liquid, like alcohol, or solid, like hashish and other such drugs.

Why has the drinking of alcohol been described as a sin? Because the drinker becomes unpleasant and detestable in his words and acts.

The teacher should state what bad effects the consumption of alcohol and similar drugs has on society, health and the economy.

Social effects. Anyone who takes drugs or alcohol becomes cut off from the people around him. He breaks away, even from his family, and always seems withdrawn into himself. If he is in the company of other people he causes a lot of problems and creates disturbances.

Effective effect. Alcohol and comparable drugs constitute a scourge financially, because the consumer spends enormous sums in order to procure them.

Damage to health. Alcohol and drugs are extremely harmful to the brain, and can even cause madness. They harm the entire body.

Second lesson

This lesson is based on the verse 'Wine, games of chance, dolmens and divining arrows are an abomination and work of the devil. Avoid them . . . perhaps you will be happy'.

Aims:

To make the pupil aware of the harm caused by alcohol and other drugs.

---

* Drug education for elementary teacher-training colleges, second year; syllabus content and teacher's guide - Institute of Education Bakht er-Ruda, Khartoum, Ministry of Education, 1982.

Steps in the second lesson:

Alcohol is one of the harmful drugs. List some items used in its manufacture. Alcohol may be prepared from dates, grapes, different types of corn, barley, etc.

Give a definition of alcohol. Alcohol intoxicates and blurs the mind.

Describe the various stages in the prohibition of wine and comparable drugs.

First verse: 'From the fruit of palm-trees and vines you extract an inebriating beverage and a delicious nutriment., This verse shows that the consumption of alcohol was permitted in earlier times.

Second verse: 'If people question you about wine and games of chance, say: They both involve a great sin and also an advantage for men, but the sin is greater than their usefulness'. This verse refers to the harmfulness of wine.

Third verse: 'O you who believe! Come not to prayer when you are drunk; thus will you know what you are saying.' This verse forbids prayer in a state of drunkenness.

Fourth verse: 'Wine, games of chance, dolmens and divining arrows are an abomination and a work of the devil. Avoid them . . . . perhaps you will be happy'. It is this verse that definitely forbids wine, describing it as a work of the devil and an abomination.

Why have wine and comparable drugs been forbidden? Because they lead to drunkenness.

What do you think of the illusion of those who drink alcohol (or who take drugs) thinking that to do so improves their reasoning faculties and increases their creative powers? They are certainly mistaken, because those who drink alcohol or take drugs often find that they cannot think (or even go mad), and one often hears of road accidents due to drunkenness.

Can alcohol be used to treat certain illnesses? Alcohol must not be used to treat illness. This is a mistaken beliefe which experience has shown to be groundless. Our orthodox religion forbids its use in illness. Thus the Prophet - may the benediction and blessing of God be with him - said, in substance, 'My people cannot find a remedy in things that they have been forbidden to touch.'

QUESTIONS

1. Why was wine (*khamr*) so named?
2. Name some sins. Would you count the consumption of wine among them?
3. Describe the various stages in the prohibition of wine and give the reasons for them.
4. What do you think of the ideas of those who drink alcohol and take drugs, thinking that to do so makes them more alert and clear-headed?
5. List the ways in which alcohol and drugs can harm society and health.
6. Explain why it is wrong to say that alcohol can be sued as a treatment for certain illnesses.

II. The alternative approach

Seminar on drug abuse, Rome 1978. Report*

A report of a seminar organized by the Red Cross and the European Scout Bureau.
Red Cross Youth teams must educate those responsible for youth just as it provides training for first-aiders.
The Red Cross plays an important role in health education for young people, parents and youth organizations.
How should drug education be integrated into Scout programmes? The Scout movement must take an interest in developing both character and social skills, in particular as concerns health.

GENERAL CONSIDERATIONS

Various opinions were experessed in the two groups (the English-speaking and the French-speaking groups) as to whether the Red Cross itself should follow a medical or social approach in work relating to the problem of drug dependence.

We can state in conclusion that the Red Cross should take into consideration both the medical and social factors as well as those factors of a psychological and human character which are connected with drug dependence.

Any action taken in this field must be adpated to the specific conditions in each country and to the possibilities of the National Red Cross Society.

RED CROSS ACTION IN THE FIELD OF PREVENTION

All information on drug dependence should be objective and scientific, avoiding sensational propaganda. The information must be adapted to the different publics addressed and should in particular be channeled through the mass media. Red Cross Youth, which lacks experience in the field of drug dependence, should orient itself toward co-operation with governmental and non-governmental organizations, such as religious institutions, youth movements, former addicts, etc. The very fact of opening up the Red Cross to the largest possible number of young people and of offering them interesting and stimulating activities in which they exercise

* Published by the League of Red Cross and Red Crescent Societies, 17 Chemin de Crêts, Petit Saconnex, CH-1211, Geneva 19, and the European Scout Bureau, Geneva, Switzerland.

responsibilities should be regarded as an extremely valuable preventive measure. Red Cross Youth must educate those responsible for youth just as it does first aiders, so as to prepare them to be capable of intervening with concrete actions in the field of prevention.

The Red Cross also plays an important role in health education for: young people, parents and youth organizations. Some countries, such as France, have provided co-ordinators for health education. Red Cross Youth teams have, at their level as well, an essential role to play in health education.

It is appropriate therefore to include in the various Red Cross teaching programmes an information programme on drug dependence in one or more of the following ways: as part of first aid courses, in health education courses and in specialized professional training.

As in the case of Czechoslovakia, the Red Cross might offer to co-operate in, or even assume responsibility for, training of medical and paramedical students with regard both to information and to actual teaching.

Every National Society has a very important role to play in the prevention of drug dependence and should devote special efforts to the matter. It should however establish more or less long-term objectives and should not be disturbed if, despite its best efforts at prevention in this field, the problems of addiction should increase in its country.

WHAT CAN THE SCOUT/GUIDE MOVEMENT DO?

Subject

How to integrate drug education into Scout/Guide programmes? into adult leader training?
What can we do for rehabilitation?

Social education

It is desirable that we teach children:
- to live together with other people;
- to have good relations with other people;
- to evaluate the actions which have already been undertaken;
- to have good relations with adults;
- to be responsible to undertake practical actions;
- to take care of other people.

Character

It is desirable that we teach children:
- to act responsibly;
- to discover new things;
- to imagine new things;
- to discover the pleasure of little things;
- to find out their own solutions to the problems they are faced with.

They must discover their solutions with the aid of other people.

Hygiene (health education)

- Take care of the body, inside and outside:
  Example: good use of medicines, good food (well balanced diet).
- To find a natural way of life:
  Example: discover nature's remedies instead of chemicals.
- We must not de dependent on modern things and modern habits:
  Example: television, alcohol, tobacco.
- To learn to use without abuse-concerning alcohol and tobacco (for heroin: you can't choose heroin, for heroin is choosing you).
- To inform the parents of younger children about the programmes of health education.

Concrete suggestions relating to age ranges

- Local situations are different - we must integrate drug education at the right moment (depending on the local situation).

Below age 10
- Information on nicotine and alcohol.
- Leaders should be good examples
  Example: read stories about nicotine and alcohol and talk about it - little theatre with a small play; use handicraft (big cigarette packs with 'why do you smoke').

- Conduct surveys: example establish a health diary:
  Discover the proper characteristics of different animals from *The Jungle Book* and see how they take care of their body (example: Bagheera needs a good nose to smell but when you smoke you can't smell well).
- Talk with children in simple way about the environment circle.

10 to 13
- Alcohol/drugs - sniffing.
- Films or slides.
- Make exhibition posters.
- Ask the local non-smoking heros (sportsmen).
- Send postcards to the government (for example: Sweden).

14 to 16
- Introduce question of soft drugs.
- Scouts and Guides should find out the necessary information and make a speech on it for parents or other Scouts and Guides.
- Invite ex-drug addicts to talk in the group.
- Start to look at the newspapers to know the attitude of the society towards the drug problem and drug addicts.
- Use a camp as starting point to discuss 'care of your body'.
- Compare the experiences of the youngsters about personal senses (by replying 'no' and 'yes' to a questionnaire concerned with using nicotine, alcohol, etc.).
- Open camps like in Norway (Scouts-Guides and non Scouts-Guides)-confrontation with another kind of life.

16 plus
- Discuss hard drugs.
- Talk with somebody who has been using drugs.
- Discuss political, economic, social and psychological reasons for drug addition.
- Talk about their attitude towards the drug addicts.
- Play role game.
- Make a slide series.

TRAINING

It is necessary to train trainers.
The leader may face two situations:
1. A boy/girl who encounters the problem of drugs:
   Example: companions who propose drugs to him/her at school. If he/she has a good relationship with his/her leader, he/she will ask for advice. In this case, the leader needs to be able to give precise information on drugs and, moreover, he must have a clear idea of his attitude towards drugs.
2. The leader wants to inform the group-more than information, he needs technical support to circulate the information better:
   Example: slides, role games, sketches.

Training in drug problems should be a part of basic courses and special courses should be provided if there are special requests.

General information about alcohol, tobacco and drug should be given during the courses (technical information, e.g. technical books, pamphlets).

- Provide technical training so that the leaders can operate the activities and also get information.
- Understand the difficulties - the older leaders may have difficulties in accepting this matter.
- More training in concrete group dynamics in order to help the leaders to handle the discussions with their members in the most effective way.
- Inform the leaders about the means of analysing their local situation.

An account of an experiment on the prevention of drug addiction in schools in an industrialized country*

This French experiment on prevention concerns teachers, pupils' parents and pupils themselves. It is part of an overall government policy against drug dependence. The schools are not alone in this action; they are supported by society.

This policy for the prevention of drug addiction in schools has several aims:

1. To take action against the use of certain legal drugs such as alcohol and tobacco on school premises.

Smoking is forbidden in classrooms and other school premises, as defined in the regulations for each school which have been adopted by vote.

No alcoholic drinks, even if their alcohol content is very low, may be kept or served in school canteens, including those for senior pupils. Until the last few years, this applied only to pupils in the first years of the secondary school - that is to say, up to 15-16 years of age.

In order to prevent children from sniffing volatile solvents, the only adhesive supplied to children by the school is paste (in primary schools it is supplied free by the municipalities). In technical schools where these solvents are used, teacher are kept regularly informed concerning the situation.

2. To train a number of adults who are in contact with the young people, and who will act as *adult support groups*. Such training will enable them to provide support for the young people and also for teachers or parents who ask for assistance.

3. To give pupils a greater sense of responsibility; the main group concerned is that of pupils who are delegates. (Pupils elect delegates to discuss their problems with the school authorities. Delegates are elected for a year, and there are generally two delegates in each class.) It is the delegates' responsibility to keep the pupils informed about their problems.

It is essential that such preventive action should be co-ordinated, so that the goals aimed at should be the same throughout France, although local conditions and specific needs should be taken into account.

The central administration adapts the government's policy on drug addiction to suit schools, and encourages its application.

Guidelines for training teachers and giving young people a sense of responsibility are tansmitted to the District Educational Authorities.

Directives about drugs, transmitted by the Official Education Bulletin, are applied at the national level.

In District Educational Authorities the officials (or mediators) responsible for each educational district transmit the national prevention policy to the schools and enlist the co-operation of voluntary personnel. They take stock of local possibilities and deal with problems connected with deviant behaviour in young people or with teacher training. They evaluate information received from schools and collate it so as to formulate new proposals, if necessary.

In school: Adult support groups are chosen from among members of the teaching, administrative and medico-social staff of the school and pupils' parents who volunteer their services. They are trained to deal with problems connected with deviant behaviour.

Pupil: Arrangements to train pupils in taking responsibility have been made in only a few educational districts.

---

* Dr Nicole Sentilhes, Relation d'une expérience deprévention des toxicomanies en milieu scolaire dans un pays industrialisé: France. Unpublished study prepared for Unesco, 1984.

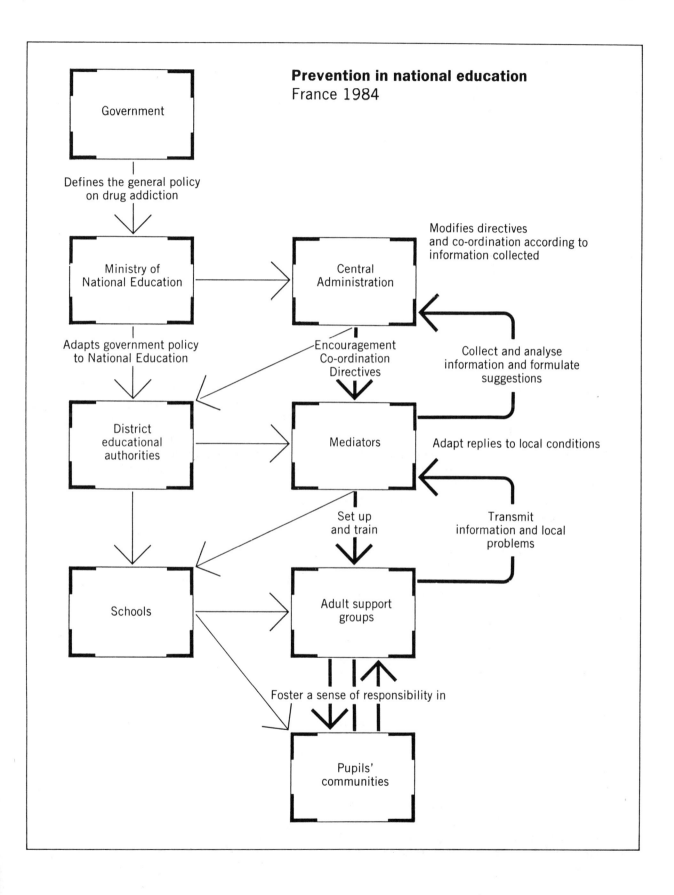

Prevention in national education
France 1984

Government

Defines the general policy
on drug addiction

Ministry of
National Education

Modifies directives
and co-ordination according to
information collected

Central
Administration

Adapts government policy
to National Education

Encouragement
Co-ordination
Directives

Collect and analyse
information and formulate
suggestions

District
educational
authorities

Mediators

Adapt replies to local conditions

Set up
and train

Transmit
information and local
problems

Schools

Adult support
groups

Foster a sense of responsibility in

Pupils'
communities

CONTENT OF TRAINING

Training of mediators (two for each educational district): Information and group work alternate, and a study is made of the Ministry's prevention policy and methods of putting it into operation.

The main subjects dealt with are:

Adolescence and the possibility of various kinds of deviant behaviour.

The occasional drug-taker and the drug addict. Arranging for treatment.

Epidemiology and drug addiction. Research in schools. Sociology and the use of drugs.

French legislation.

Possible measures for prevention in schools and in society. A written appraisal of the session has been made, and a document containing the various types of action which were suggested for mediators has been issued.

Difficulties

The main difficulties met with locally are those associated with power conflicts. Doctors, nurses, social assistants, and even parents, are sometimes very much afraid they will lose some of their authority should teachers become members of 'adult support groups'.

As young people are the main target of primary prevention, every attempt is made to exercise an influence over them. Many associations are anxious to do so, and some would very much like to take part in preventive work.

It may be necessary for them to be co-ordinated with other bodies, particularly those providing treatment, and with clubs and prevention teams, unless they play an active role in training adult support groups, which can give invaluable advice on any problems that arise.

It must be noted that some teachers prefer to be trained in such bodies, rather than in schools.

The goal and the target, however, remain the same.

A certain resistance at the adult level can be explained by the fact that relatively few young people have been trained to take responsibility.

THE ADVANTAGES OF SUCH PREVENTIVE ACTION

It takes place within the school, and uses existing structures - the teachers and other members of the school staff. It enlists the assitance of pupils' parents, who are involved in the school, through their children, and who are also members of society.

Such preventive action is not directed exclusively at the use of illegal drugs. In the adult support groups that are set up, the emphasis is placed on the possibility of improving relations between adults and adolescents, so it can prevent failure at school and many of the manifestations of disturbed behaviour in adolescents (running away from home, attempted suicide and so on). Such disturbed behaviour is itself likely to lead to drug dependence. Preventive action taken as described above avoids sending young people to specialists and cutting them off from the life of the school. Moreover, it is an attempt to make young people play an active part in improving their own health and to take a responsible attitude to their lives.

This is not a policy that is laid down once and for all; it can be modified so as to take account of suggestions made by those concerned and channelled through the mediators for each educational district.

Final report of a travelling seminar for educators and mass media specialists on problems associated with the use of drugs*

The dominating idea is that the programmes should be integrated into a global community programme, including both specific drug-centred courses and general activities, such as leisure time activities or professional training.

THREE FUNDAMENTAL NOTIONS

The Preventive Education Programme should be:
- Planned according to the situation of narcotics problem in each community.
- Integrated with other programmes in solving other social problems.
- Adjusted and changed according to the narcotics situation that changes all the time.

FIVE MAIN TARGET GROUPS AND TWO MAJOR PROGRAMMES

School-based programme
- In-school youth group (cigarettes among other substances)

Community-based programme
- Out-of-school youth
- Parents group
- Community group
- Minority group (hilltribes)
  (Information pertaining to drugs is conditioned by the availability of drugs in that situation.)

Dissemination of general knowledge about drugs to the target groups through mass media as well as government and non-government personnel dealing with public services.

The government has intended to provide profound and continual drug education to the target groups, especially the in-school youth group.

Activities such as sports, recreation, vocational training are arranged for target groups.

An intervention programme implemented in the form of consultative services (such as vocational guidance, medical and health guidance service) which can be carried out along with the School-Based Programme and the Community-Based Programme.

Prevention achievements

- Training of drug prevention personnel: a training centre set up at the ONCB to develop the capability of key personnel involved in narcotics prevention receives annually more than 150 people from various agencies concerned who participate in the training courses, such as instructors of drug prevention, co-ordinators, etc.
- Standardization of guidelines for the implementation of drug prevention consisting of curricula as well as materials for drug education and propagation for target groups.

---

* A Seminar, organized by Unesco, through the co-operation of Unesco National Commissions in the participating countries, which travelled to the Philippines, Thailand, Malaysia and Indonesia, 5-28 October 1983.

III. Indirect and selective approaches

The people's theatre in the service of prevention, Mexico*

Street theatre for the prevention of drug abuse in marginalized sections of the community. Volunteers with a knowledge of the local situation work out scenarios and staging and then act as strolling players, encouraging members of the public to take part in their performance.

OPEN-AIR COMMUNITY SOCIO-DRAMA

The team of seventeen, made up of two troupes of strolling players was set up on the initiative and under the direction of a young psychologist. It included two other specialists from the Naucalpan Local Centre; the reamining participants were volunteers living in the district where they were going to work - housewives, students and workers; most were women.

The group met regularly for a period of four months to discuss the work, think out scenarios, work out the staging and rehearse, before they went out into the streets.

WORKING METHOD

Preliminary diagnosis

When planning street theatre, one cannot find out what the 'field' is like by using the methods adopted in schools. It is more difficult, if not impossible, to survey it by means of questionnaires.

In the particular case of the Naucalpan Local Centre team, the use of volunteers from the community made it easier to find out about the local situation. Before beginning work, the group was able to study the problems met with in the district, the way of life of its inhabitants and the expressions they used.

Working out scenarios and street performances

The performances took place in the following way. The troupes went to a certain spot near a market or at a corner *pulquería*[1] at rush hour (for example, at 5 p.m., when people finish work) and put on their costumes and make-up on the spot, a means of attracting the attention of passers-by.

* Edith Massün, Utilización de técnicas de teatro popular para la prevención del abuso de drogas en comunidades marginadas, 1984. (An unpublished study prepared for Unesco.)

The stage was marked out by a white line drawn on the ground; the setting consisted of a few objects intended to give an idea of the background, for example, a table, two chairs, a street lamp; a grocery counter might be symbolized by by empty milk, pasta, gelatine, packets stuck on to a cardboard box. Make-up and costumes were meant to suggest the characters by emphasizing their features. For instance, two actresses who were playing the part of workmen put on stained overalls, safety helmets and false moustaches.

Each twenty-minute performance consisted of six to ten tableaux. The first was planned as the main centre of attraction, the scene which would decide whether the audience stayed to the end or not. So the object was to entertain the audience by showing it a lot of funny situations. At the end of the first act, an average of sixty people were watching with interest, and, since interested spectators always attract others, the audience numbered up to 300 by the end.

Some plays were mainly intended to make the audience think about the various social problems that lead to drug dependence and encourage them to play their part in finding solutions. There is virtually no set plot in a play of this kind. The main characters are two young workmen who are chatting as they leave the place where they work. The dialogues are simple - almost childish - but the point is that they refer to problems that the community has to deal with, in the language used by the community.

One of the workmen suggests that they should stop at a café before they go home, and the other replies that he doesn't drink. The first is surprised at this, and asks him why he always staggers like a drunken man when he is walking.

In this way the dialogue between the two characters brings out all sorts of basic problems: bad working conditions, malnutrition, city transport, the poor use that is made of leisure time, half of which is spent in front of the television and half at the café, and so on.

Meanwhile the narrator - there is always a narrator in plays of this kind, in order to get the audience to participate - speaks to the spectators in such a way as to encourage people to react and reply. He puts his

questions quite directly. Sometimes he seems to be speaking to children, but the spectators enter into the spirit of the thing, and they answer sincerely. 'Can anyone give me an idea? What can this young fellow do to stop poisoning himself?' or 'Do you think that someone who eats nothing but potatoes and tortillas is being properly fed? How could he improve his diet?'

At first the spectators reply jocularly: 'Why doesn't he steal!' or 'He should work harder!' But the actors take up each suggestion and improvise other dialogues around it. 'Fine! Well then, I'll do two turns one after the other next time. But you'll be worn out, and what good will it do you to fall ill with exhaustion!'

This is the sort of dialogue, over-simplified or ingenuous though it may seem, that goes down best in the parts of the community we are dealing with. Gradually the spectators take a more serious interest in the performance, and the time comes when everybody is really thinking about the problems. At almost every performance the spectators finally took part in the play; sometimes people forgot there was a 'stage', and swarmed over the white line.

The organizers hit upon the idea of setting up a workshop at the local centre for children in the community, where they could make marionnettes during the school holidays. It was run by a psychologist attached to the centre, who had taken a course in marionnette-making. Puppets made by the children, to their own design, were used for the street performances.

While working out the scenario, team members watched the children making puppets in the workshop; they noted the children's ideas about the inhalation of toxic substances and the way in which they expressed themselves, and then worked this material up into dialogues.

The team arrived at the placed selected, bearing the puppets aloft to attract the attention of the children in the street - a form of 'advertising' that never failed.

The main character in the play was a child who felt miserable and neglected by his parents, who never stopped quarrelling. Under the influence of other children, he began sniffing toxic substances. When his mother discovered this, she told his father, who began to beat him. The mother tried to protect the child, and the couple began to fight again - over the child, this time. Things seemed to be in a hopeless mess, but then a neighbour appeared; she explained to them that drug addiction is an illness that can be treated, and she advised them to take the child to the local treatment centre before it was too late.

It is one of the basic principles of educational people's theatre that spectators should look critically at their own stiuation as a result of their identification with the characters portrayed. It was surprising to see how well this principle worked when applied to people in the poorer districts.

People lingered after the performance, as if they were expecting something to happen. Many of those who had not felt confident enough to speak out during the performance went up to the actors to talk over their problems with them, ask advice, possible solutions or put forward ideas for future peformances. (Some, for instance, suggested that a play could be put on about alcoholism, showing the breakdown of the family and the various tragedies caused by the abuse of alcohol.)

NOTE

1. A bar where *pulque*, a traditional Mexican alcoholic drink, is sold.

Course for English-speaking African educators on the methodology of education concerning the problems associated with the use of drugs*

Teacher-training for English-Speaking Africans in Kenya for the struggle against drug abuse. An integrated approach of the whole population offers a better chance for success. Information, sensitization and research into teacher-training methodology.

OBJECTIVE

An integrated approach of the whole population: it offers better chances of success.

Methods: To be sent in the field in order to make an experiment instead of elaborating hypotheses around a table.

ORGANIZATION OF THE COURSE

Place: Embu, the capital of the Eastern Province of Kenya, a normal town without any specific problems.

Participants from seven countries attended the course. (Ethiopia, Ghana, Kenya, Nigeria, Sierra Leone, Sudan and Zambia). All those countries had undertaken, at various levels and stages, some actions in the field of preventive education relating to drugs within the framework of Unesco's regional programme.

Course duration: three weeks, the second week in the field.

PLANNING OF THE EXPERIMENT AND SCHEDULED ACTIVITIES

This comprised a simultaneous and integrated action for the whole of the population of the experimental area (family, school, environment).

The participants decided to split into three groups, so as to cover the Embu population: adults in general (comprising parents as well as school-leavers), primary-school pupils, secondary-school students.

The whole experiment was to start from the very beginning: the participants had to get acquainted with the environment and the living conditions of the people, the existing institutions, the curricula, etc.; decide which approach to take likely to involve best the target groups and to have an impact on them; measure this impact; and evaluate their own activities. Some participants had a feeling of insecurity at the beginning, and could not imagine what would come out of all this.

In fact, the participants were in the process of discovering the methodology for creating a methodology!

REPORT OF THE ADULT POPULATION GROUP

This group defined and assumed, among others, the following responsibilities: to create an awareness of the use and abuse of drugs; to educate adults to have self confidence without resorting to the use of drugs; and to pre-test instructional materials.

The group planned to meet adults in different settings, such as:

A maternal and child welfare clinic (women only).

The Provincial General Hospital out-patient group and the Hospital staff.

Adult literacy classes and teachers.

Students, parents and teachers.

The group met civic leaders and senior civil servants to discuss and collect relevant information and opinions.

The experiment covered a large part of the adult population through the use of posters, public address system, film shows,

---

* Held at Embu, Kenya, 17 January-3 February 1983. Paris, Unesco, 1983. (EPDAF/COURS/II)(ED-83/WS/68).

inter-personal communications, informal lectures and discussions.

DESCRIPTION OF THE ACTIVITIES

Target populations

Example: maternal and child welfare

The first target population consisted of about a hundred women at the Maternal and Child Welfare section of the Provincial General Hospital, Embu. Communication with the group of women was in Kikuyu and Kiembu.

The definition of drugs elicited from the women by the facilitators was that 'a drug is anything like *banghi* (cannabis), *miraa* (khat), *changaa* and *busaa* (strong alcohols) which, taken by a person, affects his behaviour.

Two sets of posters were shown; to reinforce the knowledge already acquired, to generate discussions. A third objective was to test the suitability of the posters in different learning situations.

Following presentation of the effects of the use of drugs, a discussion took place during which the following questions and assertations were made by the women:

Doctors know the effects and dangers of smoking, why do they keep on smoking?

What are you doing with the manufacturers of cigarettes and drinks?

It is difficult for parents to stop smoking and drinking because the doctors, who know the effects, smoke and drink.

How can we convince our husbands who drink and smoke heavily to stop?

Talk to our husbands who are more affected by the problem of abuse of drugs.

Answers by the group:

The women were advised not to copy bad examples, e.g. smoking and drinking, even when these are done by doctors.

The women were asked to dissuade their children from bad habits such as those mentioned above.

The were advised to transmit to their husbands their new knowledge on the effects of drugs.

Information was provided on the action by the Government of Kenya in prohibiting smoking in public places, proscribing brewing of local beer and spirits, and banning the advertising of cigarettes in the mass media.

Personal examples and experiences were used: a member of the Group said that his wife was able to persuade him to stop smoking.

In discussing the effects of the abuse of drugs and the ways of solving the problems associated with abuse, the following issue came up: there is a need for medical personnel to advise the government to disallow the manufacture and the sale of alcohol and cigarettes.

EVALUATION

In planning learning activities for the various groups, such as the parents of the Kangaru Primary School pupils, a variety of methods and techniques were used given the heterogeneity of the groups and certain characteristics, expecially the physical and psychosocial.

The group had set out to achieve two main objectives: to provide knowledge and understanding on drugs and to create an awareness of the effects of the use of drugs on the individual and on the community. The level of understanding was tested by the use of questions and answers: members explained the meaning of the word 'drug'. The level of awareness during the discussions (free, not directed) has been good.

Increased participation of the learners could be obtained by the use of educational songs, stories, drama or simulation exercises.

Substance abuse among the elderly*

*Specialized information on the elderly and drugs, published in Canada.
Information concerning the abuse of alcohol and medicine by the elderly*

ALCOHOL - THE MOST ABUSED

The evidence suggests, not surprisingly, that alcohol is the foremost substance of abuse by the elderly, followed by drugs obtained legally through prescriptions and over the counter. Illicit drug use is not unheard of, but its incidence is small.

'The treatment of problem drinking in elderly patients is complicated by the sometimes overwhelming variety of physical, mental, and social disturbances that go with the process of ageing,' says Dr Eloise Rathbone-McCuan, director of the Levindale Geriatric Research Center, Baltimore. At the two initial stages in particular, complications arise when indicators of alcohol abuse are mistaken for signs of senility or chronic brain symptom (CBS).

Age-specific factors such as the higher incidence of physical illness; reduced intellectual and physical capabilities; malnutrition; falls; and increased vulnerability to psychiatric disorders resulting from these and other conditions, including social isolation, economic deprivation, retirement, loneliness, boredom, the loss of loved ones, reduced sexual potency, and a sense of purposelessness can all be misread and dismissed as natural phenomena. Several studies have illuminated the similarities in symptoms between elderly alcoholics and non-alcoholics suffering deterioration of cerebral function (CBS) due to advanced age, making accurate diagnosis of alcoholism difficult for clinicians who are not well-versed in geriatrics.

The fact, too, that a large proportion of the aged live alone, without the support of family and friends and often with some physical infirmity, hampers the recognition of alcohol-related problems. Because of this, the task of detection often falls heavily on the shoulders of the 'outreach' social-service personnel and physicians.

Dr Rathbone-McCuan's estimate that one-third of the non-institutionalized population over 65 visit a doctor once a month underlines the crucial part played by the medical profession in discovering drinking problems. For those reluctant or unable to venture out on their own to seek help, the visiting public health nurse may be the only hope for detection.

NO STRICT DEFINITION

A research team at the Rutgers University Center of Alcohol Studies also warns against the tendency to apply strict definitions of alcoholism to the elderly. This derives, in part, from the theory that there are at least two distinguishable types of geriatric alcohol abuser who may have nothing in common beyond a diagnosis of alcoholism. One has a lengthy history of alcohol problems; the other began drinking heavily late in life. Although the assumption is generally made that the latter group's distress is a response to life changes brought on by ageing, Alcoholism and Drug Abuse Institute director Marc Schuckit of Seattle cautions against it. 'The vast majority of people undergoing these stresses do not develop substance abuse. Also, abuse of alcohol can intensify somatic problems, isolation, and loss of status which tend to occur in older individuals in the first place.' The co-existence of life problems with evidence of alcohol abuse does not prove a causal relationship, according to Dr Schuckit. 'There exists the same danger of assuming that because something makes sense, it is true.'

---

* By Judy Dobbie. Published by the Addiction Research Foundation, 33 Russell Street, Toronto, Canada M5S 2S1.

PEAK PERIODS OF ALCOHOLISM

A major prevalence study of alcohol problems in the community twelve years ago established that alcoholism peaks between the ages of 45 and 54 and again from 65 to 74.

It has also been acknowledged that elderly drinkers generally consume less than their more youthful counterparts. Not only do lack of money, a changed social pattern and decreased desire for alcohol combine to reduce social drinking among the elderly, but tolerance to both alcohol and drugs diminishes with the metabolic changes that accompany the ageing process. 'The chances of a person over 55 years of age being an alcoholic in the clinical sense of the word are minimal,' the Rutgers group told the Alcohol and Drug Problems Association of North America in 1973.

TROUBLE WITH ATTITUDES

Attitudes play an important, and sometimes decisive, role in diagnosis and treatment. Symptoms of alcohol abuse are frequently obscured in elderly patients admitted to hospital for treatment of acute physical ailments as a result of concealment by the alcoholics themselves or their family.

'Denial is infinitely greater in the elderly,' says Addiction Research Foundation of Ontario medical consultant Dr Sarah Saunders. 'Most of them weren't brought up to deal with their emotional problems, and they often view alcoholism as a sin.'

Many physicians and family members have come to look upon alcohol as the only pleasure left to the aged and are reluctant to regard its abuse as a problem. This attitude is probably the most common, say addiction specialists, as well as being easily the most insiduous.

'Many people refuse to see the suicidal behaviour behind much of senile alcoholism,' says gerontologist Alex Comfort from the Institute of Higher Studies at Santa Barbara. 'They don't seem to think it matters if old people are hurting themselves. Relatives often encourage elderly family members to drink because it keeps them occupied and out of the way. They fill old people with depressants like alcohol and tranquillizers to keep them quiet.'

PHYSICIANS' GUILT

This 'formidable array of drugs' also results, at least in part, from loose prescribing methods by physicians untrained in geriatrics who find it simpler to medicate the symptoms of ageing rather than treat them, or who fail to appreciate the effects of multiple drugs on the elderly. Says Vancouver psychiatrist J.C. Morrant: 'In hospitals and nursing homes, the over-prescribing is surprising. A prescription chart may list a hypnotic, an anti-psychotic or two, an anti-Parkinsonian agent, a cardiac glycoside, a form of potassium supplement, a diuretic or two, a vasodilator, an assortment of analgesics (often proprietary ones containing several ingredients), vitamins, hormones, and sometimes three different aperients. . . . This *furor therapeuticus* reflects the physician's guilt at being unable to cure the incurable.'

The hazard in such prescription techniques, according to Dr Morrant, lies in the fact that most prescription drugs and many over-the-counter drugs can cause psychiatric symptoms as a side effect in aged patients. Abuse of over-the-counter medications such as analgesics (aspirin compounds), antihistamines, anticholinergics (found in virtually all proprietary nerve remedies), and those containing bromide has been linked with depression, confusion, agitation, drowsiness, and even toxic psychosis. Surveys have found, in fact, that analgesic abuse tends to increase with age in both men and women.

CRUCIAL AND VEXING ASPECT

When prescribed in too-large or too-frequent doses, or consumed in combination with other substances such as alcohol, many drugs provoke new symptoms more onerous than the ones they were meant to alleviate. And worse, the new symptoms risk being misconstrued as further evidence of senility rather than as an adverse drug reaction.

Less-than-stringent prescription practices can also contribute to accidental and intentional overdoses among the elderly. For, as British researcher A. J. Smith says, the drugs chosen by the aged to commit suicide 'are probably dictated not by the patient's knowledge of pharmacology, but by simple availability.' This is underscored by findings which indicate more than three-quarters of suicide attempts by the elderly are made with drugs obtained from their own physicians. In their 1975 review of elderly suicide, University of Southern California School of Medicine researchers Roger Benson and Donald Brodie stressed the likelihood of physical illness existing in old people who attempt suicide. 'There is no doubt that serious physical disease is a factor in influencing a decision to take one's life at any age,' they note. In the elderly, where it is manifested most often in diseases of the cardiovascular system, it has been identified in up to 60 per cent of cases.

The acute drug reaction - whether inadvertent or deliberate - is 'one of the most crucial and vexing aspects' of drug abuse among the aged, according to sociologist David Petersen. His 1972 study of 1,128 patients admitted to Miami's Jackson Memorial Hospital with diagnosed drug overdoses showed that sedatives and minor tranquillizers were involved in four of five cases where patients were over 50. 'The significance of these drugs as causal agents in the majority of accidential overdoes and suicidal gesturing cases cannot be denied,' says Petersen. Of the thirty different medications identified as contributing to overdoses among the older group, the most frequently abused were Valium, Tuinal, phenobarbitol, and Darvon, a non-narcotic analgesic.

'Probably one in ten people over the age of 60 are drug abusers,' Marc Schuckit told the California Medical Association recently. 'Physicians should have a high index of awareness of the abuse of sleeping pills, anti-anxiety drugs, antidepressants, and stimulants in older people.' He himself feels 'very strongly' that amphetamines should never be prescribed for elderly patients, and that other mood-altering drugs should be warranted only rarely. Adds Vancouver psychiatrist J. C. Morrant: 'Barbiturates in the elderly should go the way of bromides - in the dispensary trash can.'

*Women and prescription drugs**

A Canadian tract to alert women to the dangers of taking too many prescription drugs.

DID YOU KNOW THAT . . .

Twice as many women as men receive prescription drugs.

Minor tranquillizers represent the most commonly prescribed class of drugs in Canada.

Minor tranquillizers have the ability to produce tolerance (making increased doses necessary to achieve the same effects). They can also cause psychological dependence (the drug becomes so central to the person's thoughts, emotions, and activities that it is extremely difficult to stop using it) and physical dependence (the body adapts to the presence of the drug and withdrawal symptoms occur if its use is stopped abruptly).

Minor tranquillizers can produce such unexpected effects as agitation, insomnia, aggression, rage and hostility (the symptoms for which they have been prescribed).

Minor tranquillizers are the second cause of poisonings reported in Canada.

Minor tranquillizers plus alcohol and/or other psychotropic medication (barbiturates, non-barbiturate sedatives and sleeping pills) can produce an effect greater than either drug alone would have. This could be fatal.

Abrupt cessation of minor tranquillizers after prolonged use may result in physical withdrawal symptoms - tremors, agitation, stomach cramps and sweating.

Incoordination, confusion, drowsiness, slurred speech, headache, laziness, giddiness and sleep-walking are frequent effects of excessive doses of minor tranquillizers.

BEFORE YOU TAKE A DRUG . . .

You need to discuss with your doctor:

How necessary is the drug which is being prescribed.

Why it is being prescribed for the length of time that it is.

Why it is being prescribed at the dosage that it is.

Possible interactions with food or beverages, and most importantly, with alcohol and other drugs.

Other medications you are currently taking.

What possible side effects you might expect from the drug.

What alternatives there may be to taking the drug.

Finally . . .

Make sure before you leave the doctor's office that you have discussed *all* of the questions which you had intended to ask.

CONSIDER . . .

Some stress is part of daily living. Some times are more stressful than others.

In specific situations, drugs may be useful for short periods of time, to relieve symptoms in carefully selected individuals. However, the drugs don't cure the source of anxiety, depression or sleeplessness. They may look like a short-cut to the solution of basic problems, but they are not.

Ordinary human problems which in the past were seen as part of normal life are increasingly being seen as medical problems. Since they are now seen as medical problems, we seek and are often given quick chemical 'solutions', including some prescription drugs such as minor tranquillizers.

---

* Published in 1980 by the Addiction Research Foundation, 33 Russel Street, Toronto, Canada M5S 2S1.

The drug situation in Spain*

Many people use legal drugs. They smoke, they drink, they use amphetamines and anti-depressants. Why attack young people when the drugs that we take every day openly, are often more dangerous and more harmful?

THE DRUG SITUATION

The problem is so huge that parents and educators are getting worried. In particular, there is much confusion owing to lack of knowledge about drugs and how they affect people. That is why correct information is urgently needed.

A survey of parents carried out in October 1977 in connection with the Drugs Department of the Criminology Institute of the Universidad Complutense, Madrid, produced, the following results:

Question: What would you do if your child came home drugged?

Replies:

■ 14 per cent: 'I'd try to talk to him.'

■ 63 per cent said: 'I'd flog him within an inch of his life.'
   I'd throw him out of the house.'
   I'd report him to the police.'

■ 23 per cent refused to accept the very idea that their child would take drugs.[1]

The booklet first defines terms such as drug addiction and drug dependence, and then points out the difference between occasional and habitual drug-taking.

4,000,000 drug addicts who do not break the law

Medicinal drugs and alcohol are the most dangerous drugs in Spain at present. Their abuse is increasing. And even if the police do not *charge us* and we are *not ostracized by* society, yet the drugs consumed are in many cases more dangerous than others prohibited by law, the consumption of which is illegal.

For example, in 1977 the Social Security system paid out 2,000 million pesetas for psychotropic drugs - that is, medicinal drugs for the treatment of illnesses which have nothing to do with fever, pain or the functioning of the organs of the body. They are given to some 4 million people, who take enormous amounts of tranquillizers, stimulants, sleeping pills, etc.

In the city of Madrid alone, it is estimated that between 2 and 4 per cent of the people take amphetamines regularly, and two-thirds of students at exam time.

Dependence on pharmaceutical drugs, that is, the situation of persons who take medicinal drugs that can be quite easily obtained from chemists' shops - is a serious problem in our society, yet very little is said about it. Many of those who demand extremely severe measures against those who take the 'other' drugs are themselves dependent on pharmaceutical drugs, but they maintain that the drug problem has nothing to do with them.

If, in addition to the 4 million Spaniards (and that is a bare minimum) who abuse medicines, we count 2.5 million alcoholics (and that, too, is a conservative estimate) in Spain; add those who drink coffee, smoke cigarettes and so on, we get a total of about 10 or 12 million persons who take drugs of one kind or another. Yet we point the finger at young people, as if they were the only ones, and refuse to consider the fact that the difference lies in the 'type' of drug (as well as 'legal' drugs, for which they are not criticized, they take 'illegal' drugs, which bring down wrath on their heads); and we also refuse to admit that some of the drugs that we, the righteous, take every day, openly, even making a social ritual of their

---

*   Loles Diaz Aledo, 'Las drogas a lo claro', 5th ed., Madrid, Popular, 1985.

consumption, may prove more dangerous and more harmful.

'Spaniards spent the trifling sum of 32.5 million pesetas a month on anti-depressants in 1978. (Our chemists stock eighty-eight different brands of anti-depressants.)

'Psychotropic drugs account for 70 per cent of all sales of medicines in Spain. For example, we take over 2.5 million bottles of Valium a year, at a cost of 216 million pesetas.'[2]

NOTES

1. *Extracts from: Josep Laporte i Salas, Les drogues*, Barcelona, Ediciones 62, 1976 (Monographies médiques, 13)
2. *Ciencia y pensamiento*, February 1980.

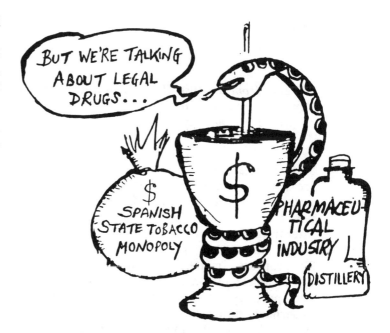

Rumours*

Extracts from an Australian sensitizing brochure.
Rumours circulate about drugs. What is the truth?
Advice. Find out precise facts in order to avoid harmful results.

Matters relating to drugs are fertile subject areas for rumour formation. Even factual material on drugs is often conflicting, research findings are open to various interpretations and there are large areas where knowledge is scarce or non-existent. To confuse matters further, drugs have different effects on different people and it is not possible to tell from someone else's experience how a drug is going to affect you. Add to all this the fact that drugs are either directly or potentially important to everyone. This introduces emotional bias, and it becomes extremely difficult to sort fact from fiction and reliable information from rumour.

Let us look at marihuana as an example. Common beliefs are that it has no harmful effects, that it leads to taking other stronger drugs and that it increases creativity. None of these common beliefs has ever been proved, but neither has convincing evidence been brought forward as disproof. There are indications that marihuana may have harmful effects and that some people who take marihuana do go on to more dangerous drugs, though more because of personality problems than as a consequence of smoking pot. As for creativity, it seems that imagination may be increased while concentration is lowered and the net effect is zero. But the evidence is not conclusive and there is still much doubt as to the actual effects of smoking marihuana, especially over a long period.

It is exactly this kind of uncertainty that gives rise to unfounded beliefs and rumours about drugs and their possible effects. While not everything is yet known about drugs, there is still plenty of information available. If we want to be in a position to decide for ourselves about drugs, and not fall prey to the wrong information that is spread in rumour form, we should find out accurate information about drugs and their effects.

While we rely to a large extent on what we 'hear' from others as a basis for our day-to-day actions, it is worth remembering that in important matters accurate knowledge is essential if we are to avoid unpleasant consequences.

POSSIBLE DISCUSSION TOPICS

1. What are some of the rumours you have heard involving drugs? How would you set about making sure that they *are* rumours?
2. If you found that a rumour was spreading among your classmates, what could you do to prevent its spreading?
3. This pamphlet has given some examples of how a newspaper report could give rise to a rumour. Can you think of other ways in which newspapers could be responsible for the creation or spread of a rumour?
4. What kind of influence do you feel that newspaper articles on drugs have on young people? You could take into consideration different kinds of reporting, e.g. sensational articles, factual articles, reports of personal experiences, articles involving popular pesonalities.
5. Would someone who had tried drugs be a source of reliable information?
6. Where would you look for accurate information on drugs? What sort of information would you collect and why?

---

* A brochure prepared by the National Information Service on Drug Abuse, P.O. Box 100, Woden, ACT 2606. Published by the Australian Government Publishing Service, P.O. Box 84, Canberra, ACT 2601, Australia.

Scenes of family life*

An extract from a special issue of a magazine for the parents of adolescents in Cologne (Federal Republic of Germany).

The object of this issue is to get parents to think about their attitudes towards their children. The different ideas of different generations should be set side by side and discussed. Parents should avoid being too dictatorial about their children's future; they should try to understand how their children differ from them, discuss things with them more, and show them more affection.

Parents are faced with fresh problems when their children reach adolescence. Many parents are themselves going through a critical period (the forties and fifties) and are taking a fresh look at their marriage relationships and their working future. The children's behaviour upsets them, and misunderstandings and arguments become more and more frequent. The children want more independence; they demand that their rights be respected, but they won't hear of duties. Their friends and the discothèque mean more than anything else to them - at least, so it seems. Some of them smoke, drink or have tried other drugs. There is only one way of making things easier, and that is to seize every opportunity to talk to the children, to one's spouse and to one's relations who are having difficulties, about the worries of daily life and about future prospects.

This issue is intended for the parents of children aged between 13 and 17.

How are things in your family?

Parents and children have different ways of looking at situations and different opinions about them.

Children and parents are asked to reply separately to a questionnaire, which is the same for both, and then to compare their replies. The questions are about the way the children dress, their school results, their wanting to spend the night with friends, what they are planning to do later on, the fact that the parents don't know who their children's friends are, the hashish that is passed around at school, and the fact that the parents drink and smoke a good deal.

Parents and children then explain their points of view, for the replies are different more often than not. A simple conversation such as this can avoid misunderstanding and tension.

DECISIONS ABOUT THE FUTURE

Is school the parents' business or the children's?

Many parents see their child's difficulties at school as their own fault. The best thing to do is to try to find the cause of the difficulties by discussing them with the teacher and the child (material problems, problems related to puberty and so on). A parents' meeting is a good chance to talk about them, for many parents have to face the same difficulties.

It is most important that the child should take part in the discussion of his difficulties, for we all put a decision into practice more readily if we have had a say in it.

We want our child to succeed in life

The result of the parents' ambition for their child is usually that they want him to succeed at school and in a career (and to do better than his father).

---

* 'Familien Scenen'. Bundeszentrale für gesundheitlich Aufklärung, Postfach 910152, 5000, Köln 91, Federal Republic of Germany. Published by courtesy of the Federal Centre for Health Education in Cologne.

That is understandable; but ambitious parents may exert such pressure on the child that he shows signs of stress (headaches, difficulties in sleeping, nervousness, depression, listlessness and so on).

Another difficulty can arise when the parents are determined to choose their children's future occupation, in order to fulfil an ambition in which they themselves have failed or an aspiration they have not achieved, taking no accout of his inclinations or his abilities. Over-work at school can make a child sick, incite him to use drugs to get away from his troubles, or lead to other behavioural disorders (500 pupils commit suicide every year, and it is not known how many such suicides are due to stress at school).

At the other end of the scale there is the child of whom too little is expected; he too is in danger. He may explore other ways of gaining attention - and one way may be drugs.

FIRST SWEETS,
THEN DRUGS AND CIGARETTES

Lastly, it must be said that the practice of accustoming children to passive behaviour with regard to eating is characteristic of our times. Such behaviour begins when the child is very young - for example, when a baby's crying is thought to express a wish for food rather than an appeal for help or a need for companionship. On the whole, it is much less trouble to quieten a child by giving him a sweet or a plaything than to do something about him.

When a young child has learnt to satisfy his needs for praise and trust, love and physical contact by means of food and sweets, the chances are that later on he will turn to them to fill the place of what he has not got. And he will often turn to other 'dummies'-cigarettes, alcohol, or even drugs.

Many parents forget that their children need to be kissed and cuddled even when they are grown up. And the children, even when they are grown up, need real evidence that their parents are concerned about their worries and their problems.

Voices from a far corner - Burma*

Alerting Parents. Transcript of a group session composed of six adults (five married and with children), all over 40 and from well-informed circles. They analyse the different factors contributing to taking drugs, information problems and the role of parents.

They come to see me every Sunday. Just a group of six. Except for one who is beginning to become an 'old bachelor', all are married and young parents, having one or two children some of whom are high school students. Their average age is 42, the old bachelor being the oldest at 47. The youngest is 30, newly married. Among them is a woman, wife of one of the group; she and her husband are of the same age, just over forty. They are all university graduates, fairly well employed, well read, well informed and keenly interested in social problems.

Recently, one Sunday, I gave them a subject for discussion, the one they are all concerned about: *the drug problem.*

'You all must have read and heard about the drug problem,' I said. 'As you know, it has become a very serious problem, and governments and non-governmental organizations of the world are busy taking preventive and protective measures against drug dependence and drug trafficking. Now let me have your opinion, the common man's opinion.'

'Of course, there are several factors. The one that is right under my nose is drug availability. I refer to the drug retailing business. Street-corner betel stalls are selling narcotic cigarettes to high school students. The young fellows smoke the cigarettes just before they go into their classes and also in the interval and after the classes. I don't want to talk about drug trafficking carried on as a Big Business by drug kings in other parts of the world that we haved read about in news magazines and journals. And I am not ambitious to offer solutions to this worldwide problem. All I want to suggest is, please take drastic action against this small-scale retailing business. If that is done we'd be saving a lot of our youngsters from dreaded drug dependence,' the old bachelor said.

'Ko Bo Gyi has hit the mark. Young people's natural curiosity about drugs leads them to try the stuff just for fun. Their curiosity is aroused by propaganda. Of course, the propaganda is aimed at drug abuse. It's meant to inform people, especially young people, about the various drugs, their properties and effects; how harmful these effects are, and what measures are being taken by authorities. But the pity of it is that youngsters are fascinated by the initial effects of the drugs, such as excitability, euphoria and some such things. They usually ignore the consequences of drug dependence,' Aung Tha Lin said slowly and carefully.

'I think you have a point there,' said Maung Zaw. 'Propaganda is well-intentioned and commendable but sometimes it hits the wrong target. Sometimes it serves to prompt rather than deter. Young people are so weak against temptation. They have heard so much about drugs and their curiosity has been aroused, and at that time propaganda comes in to feed them with the facts of drugs, such as initial effects of courage, of course Dutch courage, euphoria, diminished feeling of fatigue, sensation of increased muscular strength and so on. These things unwittingly push the callow youth to the drugs.'

'Ko Zaw is right. Propaganda often hits the wrong target, or I'd say, misses the right one,' said Ma Win Kyi, an office-worker who has a son reading in a high school class. 'But I'm sure the root lies in home-life. An

* By Tek Toe, published by U Khin Maung Ayo, Secretary, Mooyit Magazine Committee, Central Committee for Drug Abuse Control and printed by the Ministry of Information, Burma 1985.

unhappy home drives the youngster from his home, and he spends most of his time out with companions, and the company he keeps is usually the bad one. Sort of birds of a feather flock together. I have a son in his mid-teens, and I have to be careful to make him happy at home. His father helps him a lot,' she said, turning to her husband, Kyaw Win, sitting by her side. Kyaw Win smiled back.

'Yes, I know from personal experience that home-life is most important in bringing up children. Parents are the key persons; they are the first teachers, as we say in Burmese. If they fail in their duty as parents, their children's lives will surely go to pieces,' he said.

'Of course, an unhappy home is the breeding ground of all ills, socially, psychologically and morally. Children's future depends on their parents. Some parents are themselves so disorganized and disoriented that they easily set bad examples to their children. There are also some who are too busy to look after their children or too stupid to be able to manage them properly. Discipline is apparently getting to be obsolete in modern society. Modern men and women tend to equate discipline with restriction: a deterrent to personal freedom. And, naturally, their children are at loose ends,' Tha Sein said with a slight sigh.

'Now, about this availability again. Of course, it's easy for one to take the thing that's handy. In the case of narcotics, however, availability comes hand-in-hand with temptation. Drugs are not only made available but they are made attractive to young people whose curiosity is aroused. Temptation is made by bad company and touts. Persuasion plays its role. Young people want to be different; they want to take a different road; to them that means fun and adventure. They ache to try; they want to know what drugs really are; they wish to take a trip into psychedelic world. First, just a pinch, just a try, but trying moves on and on until at last they are entrapped. A sad story,' Win Thein Myint remarked.

'Oh, yes that's human perversity. Perversity is more pronounced in young people,' said Kyaw Win. 'It's blended with defiance. If you say don't do it, the youngster will do it purposely, just to show defiance to authority. I want to warn elders to avoid saying 'don't'. Restriction does more harm than good. Young people, especially teenagers, are very difficult to handle. Their arrogance is as large as their ignorance. Few parents are equal to the task. A lot of patience and understanding is called for, and most parents lack them. Some of them are as immature as their children; so, how can you expect any confidence or even respect from their children?'

'It's sad but true,' said Tha Sein. 'Most modern men and women are not well fitted to be parents. They themselves are victims of unhealthy social and moral conditions of modern life. Wonderful things have been created by science and technology, but it is regrettable that scientific progress gradually subtracts moral values some of which are fast disappearing. I think it's Albert Schweitzer who said that man is becoming a superman, thanks to science and technology, but he has failed to raise himself to the level of reason which should correspond to his possession of superhuman strength.'

'Lowering of moral standards is responsible, I think, for the flourishing of corruption. Corruption, corruption everywhere! How do these drug kings have their consignments of drugs transported to the markets? They pave their way with money. First, they pay good prices for raw materials, and the cultivators are encouraged to grow more. In South America, news magazines say, farmers are much better off than ever before for their cultivation of coca plants. To them, as to many others, money and not, repeat not, morality is important. They say they've got to live, and they need money, not morality. They look up to drug Mafia bosses who throw money about to get what they want,' said Maung Zaw.

Win Thein Myint said with a chuckle: 'This reminds me of the escape of Utena in the legends. The captured king made his escape on an elephant. Enemy troops pursued him, and when one troop got near him, he strewed gold and silver coins. The soldiers forgot their mission and stooped to grab the coins while Utena's elephant made the distance. Greed and corruption - mankind's incurable diseases!'

'Yes, corruption is rife everywhere; it has become more widespread and more shamelessly daring after the Second World War, I think. Easy money! Lure of the lucre! Only very few can resist it. It's sad to see morality being pushed into limbo. Morality has become an old-fashioned idea relished only by old fogeys. Modern man feels rather uncomfortable about morality,' said Maung Zaw.

With a short laugh, Win Thein Myint parodied: 'Oh, morality, where are the charms/That sages have seen in thy face?'

Smiles and chuckles.

'Morality is no laughing matter. It's a serious point in any discussion of the drug problem,' said Bachelor Bo Gyi. 'Morality makes man human. It's because morality is fading out in modern society that a lot of scourges such as drug abuse have sprouted out as complex and insoluble problems. I'd say narcotics is as serious and deadly as nuclear weapons. Ways and means may be found to reduce, if not wipe out, nuclear weapons but narcotics can't be curbed so effectively, for the simple reason that it's a personal problem assuming international dimensions.'

'I agree with you,' said Tha Sein. 'Nobody can solve this problem unless the individual concerned reforms himself or herself. Other people can only organize public opinion against drug abuse. The person concerned must mend his ways. International undertakings are all right, but every individual must refuse to take to drugs; otherwise, all grandiose plans and campaigns would fall through.'

'Parents must do their best to look after their children with love and thus earn their respect and confidence,' Ma Win Kyi reiterated. 'I must say again and again that unhappy and broken homes are at the bottom of the drug problem. It's said that charity begins at home. Lack of charity in the sense of charitable acts and attitudes would spawn evil at home.'

Kyaw Win said: 'About good and bad company, I think youths should be properly organized, I mean organized informally and intimately, and given practical lessons in good companionship and good behaviour. They should also be encouraged to read wholesome writings so that they may learn to think.

They will then be able to see reason and tell good from bad. Young people should be kept busy with entertaining and at the same time profitable pursuits. They should learn to do hard labour in the service of the state and the people; in other words, they should learn to live for others.'

'Very good idea. It can be turned into practice. About the organization of youths, we all support the activities of Lanzin Youth Organization. What Ko Kyaw Win means to say is promotion of camaraderie among the youths. Of course, that can be done within the scope of Lanzin Youth's activities, but what Ko Kyaw Win wants to emphasize is that besides formal contacts youths should be encouraged to make more friends, good friends who help one another. They can, and should, use their influence and persuasion to get erring ones to mend their ways. The words of peers carry more weight than the words of superiors and elders.'

Rounding up the discussions, I made the concluding remarks:

'You have given your views on this very serious problem which touches the lives of people. But I'm afraid it's almost insoluble because it's so complex, but we must not give up. We must go on fighting even if we know we are fighting a losing battle. And we, the common men, can only mend our fences and fortify our homes. The forces of evil are present everywhere, and if every family could protect itself by being always on the alert, I think the battle would be won. Let's hope that tomorrow will be better.'

There is nothing wrong with medicines, but they can be wrongly used*

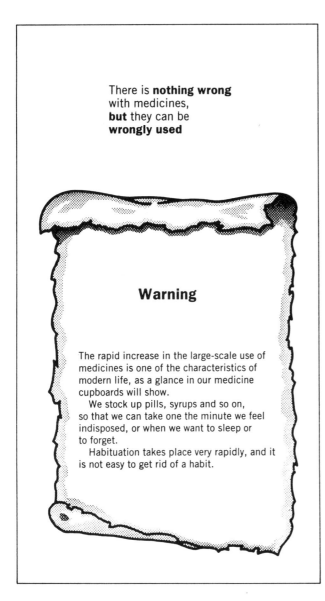

There is **nothing wrong**
with medicines,
but they can be
wrongly used

Warning

The rapid increase in the large-scale use of
medicines is one of the characteristics of
modern life, as a glance in our medicine
cupboards will show.
  We stock up pills, syrups and so on,
so that we can take one the minute we feel
indisposed, or when we want to sleep or
to forget.
  Habituation takes place very rapidly, and it
is not easy to get rid of a habit.

Your baby

doesn't sleep
cries
stops his parents from sleeping

- **a soothing syrup?**
- **a suppository?**
- **a pill?**
that you used
for your first baby.

NO

It may not be a good thing to give him
medicine without a doctor's advice.
  It's better to give him a little affection,
a lot of love and a bit of time, or even to
sing to him, however badly.

---

* 'Les médicaments ne sont pas mauvais, mais il peut y avoir une mauvaise façon de s'en servir'. A pamphlet produced
by the Centre d'Accueil et d'Aide aux Toxicomanes (Reception and assistance centre for drug addicts), 26 rue du
Maréchal de Lattre de Tassigny, 78100 St Germain en Laye, and 23 bis rue Jean Mermoz, 78000 Versailles. Partial use
has been made of the report of the study mission on drug problems by Mme Pelletier.

Your son
Your daughter
complains of:
a headache
pains in the legs
stomach pains...
pains anywhere

- **a soothing syrup?**
- **a suppository?**
- **a pill?**

that your neighbour
has advised.

NO

Perhaps he is worried about how he'll
get on at school next day.
Perhaps he is jealous of his new little
brother.
Perhaps he wants to **talk**.

If you don't help him to put up with
a little discomfort, what will he be able
to put up with later on?

You use pills, syrups,
suppositories
automatically and
without justification

Then
Why shouldn't your children think:
'All you need do is take...'

and when you look
in your medicine cupboard...

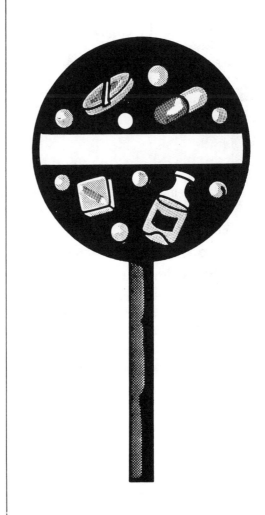

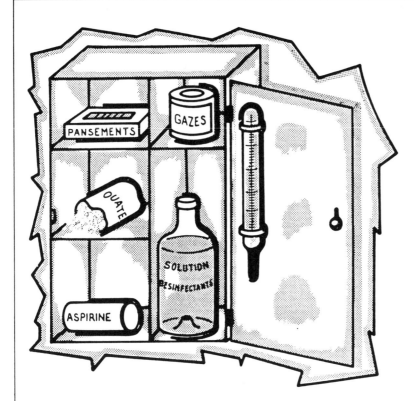

All firms make an **Inventory**. Why don't you? **Regularly**.
- Are you sure that the medicine you have taken today will be safe to take tomorrow
- Are you sure that the medicine that has been prescribed for your neighbour is not dangerous for you?
- Did you know that a syrup becomes oxydized in a few weeks once the bottle has been opened?

Every medicine is prescribed for a particular case, at a particular time, in a particular dose. Apart from any treatment you are following at present, **your medicine cupboard should contain:**

Aspirin, Gauze, Dressings, Disinfectant, Cotton wool, Thermometer

However, don't hesitate to consult your doctor or your chemist; they will give you good advice about what your medicine cupboard should contain.

IV. Three experiments evaluated

*Preventive education experiment in the field of use of drugs by young people**

An evaluation of the impact of a drug abuse prevention programme carried out in twelve primary and secondary schools in the Manilla region, of the Philippines.

In the early 1970s, preventive education came in the form of lectures, symposia, and other drug information-giving strategies on the dangers of drugs, the legal and social consequences of drug use, the pharmacological components of drugs and the penalties imposed on drug use, illegal drug manufacturing, selling, and trafficking. The prevailing philosophy during this period was, people will not use drugs if they are aware of its dangers and harmful effects to man and society. The highly legal and moral approach to drug education is very much in evidence in the Dangerous Drugs Act of 1972, which provides that 'instructions on the adverse effects of dangerous drugs, including their legal, social, and economic implications shall be integrated into the existing curricula of all public and private schools, whether general, technical, vocational or agro-industrial'.

It was observed during this period that in spite of the intensive implementation of the above-mentioned provision of the law, the number of young people being arrested for drug-related offences continued to rise. It was believed by some educators that teaching young people about drugs and their effects is counter-productive since it tends to arouse curiosity and leads to experimentation.

However, the dearth of research in this area failed to prove this assumption, hence the legal-moral approach continued to be utilized as the main strategy in the education system.

The staffing of the Secretariat of the Dangerous Drugs Board with a multi-disciplinary team of professionals, composed of psychiatrists, psychologist, social workers, educators, and lawyers, and the establishment of a Division of Preventive Education and Community Information, as one of the technical divisions of the Board, led to the search for more rational policies and educational strategies that will effectively deal with the problem of drug abuse. Findings of researches conducted in more advanced countries, and reports of international conferences on preventive education served as invaluable references for the development of innovative educational programmes. Attempts were also made to look into the needs and problems of young people confined in treatment and rehabilitation centres, as revealed in their case histories, in order to identify the underlying causes of the problem of drug use.

The need to involve other agencies as well as decision-makers in the development of educational programmes based on the

* Based on an unpublished study by Aurora S. Cudal written for Unesco in 1984.

psychosocial approach and which will be more responsive to the interests, needs, and problems of young people was keenly felt. Hence, the Dangerous Drugs Board with the collaborations of the Colombo Plan Bureau organized in 1974 a National Workshop on Drug Abuse Prevention Education. This was attended by fifty representatives from both governmental and non-governmental organizations concerned with education, social services and development, community development, youth development, health, and law enforcement. The workshop was able to avail itself of a consultant from Unesco.

The participants in this National Workshop on Drug Abuse Prevention Education formulated an Integrated Plan of Action on Drug Abuse Prevention Education, which was presented and finally adopted by the Dangerous Drugs Board as a guide in the development of educational policies and programmes.

Several teachers' guides were drafted. Rigorously controlled research allowed a serious evaluation of the drug abuse prevention education strategies and materials in twelve elementary and secondary schools.

The experiment conducted in elementary schools gave the following results:

An experiment to test the efficacy of the designed strategies and support materials was conducted.

A comparison between the post-test results with those of the pre-test results show positive changes in the personality, attitudes, and behaviour of the experimental group as compared with the control group: the percentage of pupils that showed introversion tendencies, anxiety problems and with delinquency problems decreased compared with the control class.

Pupils in the experimental class had a very high perception of values such as self-discipline, spiritual values, self-awareness, self-reliance, respectfulness and understanding. While pupils in the control classes perceived their values related to the above as average or low.

The drug-abuse-prevention programme proved equally efficient in secondary schools. It revealed significant improvement on the personality of the students, their values, their attitudes and behaviour.

Preventing young people from smoking: an educational intervention at school*

A Canadian evaluation of an approach based on the recognition and counteraction of the influence of parents and friends who smoke and of advertising that encourages smoking.

'Smoking has now been identified as the main cause of death from cancer in the United States' (Schweiker, 1982). There is now no doubt that it is the principal target to aim at if we are to ensure the primary prevention of a constantly increasing number of diseases.

The number of adults who smoke in North America may be starting to decline, but that is not true of adolescents. In Canada, 15 per cent of boys and 20 per cent of girls aged 14 smoked in 1978; and over a quarter of boys and girls aged 17 did so. There has been no change to speak of since then (Ableson et al., 1983).

A number of research workers have concentrated on programmes for prevention, because there are many arguments for them: (a) more young people can be reached by such programmes; (b) prevention is better than the difficult process of stopping smoking; (c) smoking even for a short time can be harmful for one's health (Schweiker, 1982).

The studies carried out in Quebec (Laforest, 1975; Tremblay et al., 1981; Steinberg and Saucier, 1982), together with American studies (Evans, 1976; McAlister et al., 1979; Botvin and Eng, 1982) have shown that steps must be taken at the age of about 11 or 12, at which time experimental behaviour ceases.

Until very recently, most strategies for prevention have been a failure. In 1976, Evans' team in Houston tried out a new approach to the problem in schools, based on the recognition and counteraction of the influence of parents and friends who smoke and of advertising that encourages smoking. Because of the promising results of their pilot study (Evans, 1976), a number of American research workers began to tackle the problem on the same lines; they succeeded in demonstrating the validity of interventions based on these ideas and carried out in schools among pre-adolescents (McAlister et al., 1979; Hurd and Johnson, 1980; Perry, 1980; Botvin et al., 1980).

An experiment largely based on this American approach to the problem, but adapted to suit conditions in French-speaking Canada, was carried out at Sherbrooke, in Quebec. The pilot study was made in the school year 1982/83; it covered about a hundred pupils in the first two years of the secondary course in a public school.

GENERAL AIMS

1. To foster attitudes which will help the pupil to resist the incitement to smoke that he receives from his peers, well-known adults and advertising.
2. To enable the pupil to resist the influence of his peers who smoke in his presence.
3. Four meetings were held, dealing with six experimental classes; the educational programme was: (a) the influence of advertisements for cigarettes; (b) the influence of well-known adults and of peers; (c) techniques for resisting the influence of people who smoke in the pupil's presence; and (d) personal choice.

The control group consisted of six classes in another school. Alain Rochon describes the tools used for measuring data and the detailed results of the study, and then analyses the situation as follows.

Taking only statistically significant differences between the results in the

* Alain Rochon, Prévenir l'usage du tabac chez les jeunes: une intervention éducative en milieu scolaire, 'Psychotropes', Vol. II, No 1, Winter 1985, pp. 47-54. The author is a medical consultant in health education in the Department of Public Health, Laval, Quebec, Canada.

experimental group and the control group as valid:

1. The number of pupils who started smoking between the beginning and the end of the intervention - over 10 per cent of each group in a four-month period - suggests that the first two years of secondary school are crucial in deciding whether a pupil starts smoking or not.
2. The efficacy of the strategies employed was not demonstrated at the final stage, that of behaviour (9 per cent began smoking).
3. The presence of smokers in the pupil's immediate environment has a marked effect on the efficacy of the strategies employed at the behavioural stage (9 per cent began smoking).
4. Only one aim was fully attained: the development of techniques for resisting the influence of tobacco.

If non-significant differences between results are also taken into account, we find that:

1. Such differences nearly always favour the group which has been the subject of prevention intervention, i.e. the experimental group.
2. If we look at the ultimate aim - the decision to start smoking or not - we shall see that such differences in favour of the experimental group are to be observed particularly in: (a) all the pupils; (b) girls; (c) pupils in the first year of secondary school; and (d) pupils who have no relation or friend that smokes.
3. It may be assumed that girls, pupils in the first year of secondary school and pupils who are in contact with few smokers or non are the sub-groups that are the most receptive to the strategies employed in this study.

We think that these results are, on the whole, quite promising, especially since there were two circumstances that militated against success: first, the intervention lasted a very short time (four sessions, each of seventy minutes' duration); second, the pupils in the experimental school were subject to the influence of tobacco to a greater extent, because they were allowed to smoke in the playground and also because they could buy tobacco near the school.

REFERENCES

Ableson, J.; Paddon, P.; Strohmenger, C. 1983. *Perspectives sur la santé*, Statistiques Canada.

Botvin, G. J.; Eng, A. 1982. The Efficacy of a Multi-component Approach to the Prevention of Cigarette Smoking. *Preventive Medecine*, Vol. 11, pp. 199-211.

Botvin, G. J.; Eng. A.; Williams, C. L. 1980. Preventing the Onset of Cigarette Smoking through Life Skills Training. *Preventive Medicine, Vol. 9*, pp. 135-43.

Evans, R. I. 1976. Smoking in Children: Developing a Social Psychological Strategy of Deterrence. *Preventive Medecine*, Vol. 5, pp. 122-7.

Hurd, P. D.; Johnson, C. A., 1980. Prevention of Cigarette Smoking in Seventh Grade Students. *Journal of Behavioral Medecine*, Vol. 3, pp. 15-28.

Laforest, L. 1975. *Exploration des facteurs déterminant le degré d'exposition de la population étudiante au tabagisme: rapport final*. Département des Sciences de Sherbrooke.

McAlister, A.; Perry, C.; Maccoby, N.; 1979. Adolescent Smoking: Onset and Prevention. *Pediatrics*, Vol. 63, pp. 650-8.

Perry, C. L. 1980. Modifying Smoking Behavior of Teenagers: A School-based Intervention. *American Journal of Public Health*, Vol. 70, pp. 722-5.

Schweiker, R. S. 1982. *The Health Consequences of Smoking: Cancer. A Report of the Surgeon General*. Rockville, Md., United States Department of Health and Human Services, Public Health Services, Office on Smoking and Health.

Steinberg, M.; Saucier, J. F. 1982. Un adolescent averti . . . n'y change rien: notes de recherches. *Carrefour des affaires sociales*, No. 4, pp. 38-40.

Tremblay, J.; Bibeau, G., et al. 1981. *Les mécanismes de reproduction du tabagisme chez les pré-adolescents québécois: Document de travail*. Quebec, Université Laval.

*Heroin misuse campaign evaluation: report of findings**

This study, carried out by the Research Bureau Ltd (RBL) in the United Kingdom, was designed to quantify the effects of the government's campaign upon attitudes towards heroin/drugs. This study was limited in scope to effects upon young people and parents with particular emphasis on the main target of the entire campaign, young people aged 13-20 years old. The research, like the campaign, was limited to England and Wales.

The effects of anti-heroin abuse advertising and publicity during spring/summer 1985 on young people were studied by means of two surveys in England and Wales, each of over 700 young people timed to be before and after the advertising campaign. In the event there was considerable publicity and media debate at the time of the first study.

Between the two stages the campaign was seen in all ITV areas in England and Wales and there was continuing publicity and media coverage of the topic at various times. There could be no control area without advertising, in the sense of omitting the television advertising from those of the surrounding publicity. Conclusions on the campaign and the changes created during the campaign period were reached but these changes cannot be unequivocally attributed to the campaign alone.

Overall, at the second stage 95 per cent of the young people interviewed were aware of a campaign against heroin abuse. The claimed awareness of the different media campaigns were (including prompted responses): television 80 per cent; posters 64 per cent; newspapers 56 per cent; magazines 47 per cent. Significant improvements had been found between stages for increased awareness of the symptoms/health consequences of heroin usage; decreased beliefs that taking heroin via smoking or sniffing is less addictive; increased belief in death as an inevitable consequence of heroin usage; decreased likelihood of accepting an offer of heroin made by a friend; more confident specific reasons given in support of refusal. In addition, at the second stage respondents were more likely to turn to their

parents for help about drugs. This may be a sampling effect of the results of publicity showing concerned parents.

Findings in the study would suggest that the major factors determining potential exposure to drugs are initially more 'situational' than attitudinal. Age and nature of social life are probably the factors which initially bring people close to drugs. Attitudes, reflecting psychological state, are likely to influence how they react once in contact. Overall, publicity has had a significant effect on attitudes to heroin during the summer of 1985. The high salience of the advertising campaign and the specificity of some of these effects to issues featured in the campaign suggest that advertising may have played a major part in this.

The effects of the campaign on parents were assessed by two Omnibus surveys of over 600 parents of children aged 10-20; as with the research among young people, the two stages were conducted in February/March and September/October 1985.

Awareness of publicity and editorial coverage was high at both stages among parents. In terms of the whole campaign, that is, including all advertising, awareness was reasonably high bearing in mind the relatively low exposure of the specific Parents' advertising and the precise media targeting of the Young People's campaign. Thus, at Stage II, claimed prompted awareness figures were 63 per cent for television advertising and 51 per cent for newspapers/magazines. The Young People's campaign had the greatest impact and exposure, even among parents, as illustrated

---

* Published by the Research Bureau Ltd (RBL), P.O. Box 203, Brewhouse Lane, London E1 9PA, United Kingdom.

by the much higher levels of recognition for the Young People's advertisements when shown. This finding demonstrates the degree in overlap of media consumption between parents and their children, and the difficulty of targeting a campaign to cover one group adequately yet exclude another altogether.

Only 19 per cent of parents were even vaguely aware that the leaflets were available, and only 11 per cent recognized any when shown. Response was even lower among working-class parents.

In terms of effects upon attitudes, these were generally few in number and moderate in size, although any movements were generally positive. Overall attitudes towards drugs were little changed, although a significantly lower proportion of parents agreed that their children would 'never try hard drugs', and there were a number of directional changes. Less positively large numbers of parents felt that they didn't know enought about drugs, although this fell slightly at Stage II, to 58 per cent.

Finally, the most frequent claimed reaction of parents if heroin abuse was discovered would be to seek authority - doctors, teachers drug clinics/counsellors, but not the police. Few admitted that they would get angry or over-react, and the campaign does not appear to have induced an atmosphere of panic among parents.

In conclusion, publicity had a small (albeit positive) effect among parents, despite the high visibility of the campaign among this group.